S MEXICO 1968 OLYMPIC
JRDLES FINAL MEN'S 400

OMEGA OMEGA OMEGA OMEGA OMEGA OMEGA OMEGA

The publishers and author wish to
thank the following photographers,
publications and agencies who have
contributed many of the pictures used
in this book: *Athletics Weekly*, Tony
Duffy, Ed Lacey, Paul Popper Ltd.,
Radio Times Hulton Picture Library.
Thanks are also due to the
members of the National Union of
Track Statisticians who have helped to
compile the hundreds of facts and
figures, and especially to Mr. Bob
Sparks.

Colour processing by Colour Craftsmen Ltd.
Chelmsford
Printed and bound by Jarrold & Sons Ltd.
Norwich

ATHLETICS
SPORTSGRAPH

The Marquis of Exeter, President of the I.A.A.F. since 1946, opens the European Championships. In the 1928 Olympics, as Lord Burghley, he won a gold medal for the 400 metres hurdles

I feel sure that this book, prepared in consultation with the British Olympic Association, will be of great interest to all followers of athletics, particularly in the field of the Olympic Games. The remarkable improvement in performances over the years has been a fascinating subject, and prompts speculation as to when, if ever, we will reach the ultimate record.

Harold Abrahams, whom I saw win his Gold Medal in Paris in 1924, has not only devoted much of his life to the development of athletics, but he has also made a life study of their statistics, and no-one is more fitted to marshal and edit them and delve into some of the reasons for the astonishing improvements.

I commend this book therefore to all readers and feel sure that they will find it as fascinating as I have.

THE MARQUIS OF EXETER, K.C.M.G., LL.D.

ATHLETICS
SPORTSGRAPH

MUNICH 1972

An official publication of the British
Olympic Association published by
Young World Publications Ltd

Harold Abrahams C.B.E.

Harold M. Abrahams was almost born wearing running shoes. He won his first gold medal when he was ten, and climaxed a brilliant athletics career at the 1924 Olympic Games in Paris, where he won the gold medal for the 100 metres in the then Olympic record time of 10·6 sec. As President of the Cambridge University Athletic Club, Life Vice-President of the Amateur Athletic Association and Chairman of the British Amateur Athletic Board, he has done as much as anyone to promote and support British athletics; while as a B.B.C. commentator and regular correspondent for the *Sunday Times* for over forty years, he has done much to increase public interest in the sport. The picture shows him during the 1966 Commonwealth Games in Jamaica with one of the greatest Olympic champions ever, Jesse Owens

Created by Desmond Marwood
Layout and typography by Ray Fishwick
Edited by Alan Blackwood

YOUNG WORLD  PRODUCTIONS
LIMITED
LONDON

Contents

Introduction

Top: The Olympic flame at Melbourne. Ron Clarke carried the torch into the stadium

Above: Taking the Olympic Oath in Tokyo on behalf of all the competitors — "to compete for the glory of sport"

It all started in Athens on the afternoon of Monday, April 6th, 1896. After the opening ceremony, a contemporary chronicler thus described the 100 metres of the first modern Olympic Games:

"The champions for the first race made their entrance by a subterranean passage; they were lightly attired in a flannel shirt, short under-garments and light canvas shoes. Each one was distinguished by bearing a number on his breast. As there were 21 competitors, and as they could not very well run at the same time, it had been thought advisable to divide them into three groups. The interest of the public was fully excited when the Champions entered the lists. After they had ranged themselves in a straight line, ready to bounce forward, a pistol shot gave the signal for starting. Onwards they ran, Mr. Lane, an American, arrived first at the goal, having run the race in 12 1/5th. sec."

Ten countries sent "representatives", if one may use that description of the sixty or so competitors in the twelve track and field events, since the majority of them entered privately, some on the very day of the competition. But from this humble sports meeting grew, over the next seventy years, the greatest athletics spectacle in the world, and the pattern for all modern international athletics.

Let us look at the position of athletics in 1896. England had organised national athletics championships since 1866, the U.S.A. since 1876, New Zealand since 1887, Australia since 1893 and South Africa since 1894. So far as national governing bodies were concerned, the Amateur Athletic Association of England had been founded in 1880, a New Zealand body in 1887, and one in the U.S.A. a year later. Belgium and Canada founded similar bodies in 1889, South Africa and Sweden in 1895. In other words, when the Olympic Games opened in 1896 there were only seven countries with amateur athletics governing bodies — there are now nearly 150 affiliated to the International Amateur Athletic Federation.

The rules governing competition were extremely few. The A.A.A. laws for competition occupied six pages, together with what were called "recommendations", which covered another four. Today the A.A.A. Rules for Competition occupy sixty pages. The rules for records were simplicity itself, providing that "the time must be taken by one or more competent timekeepers, the watch or watches must be proved to be accurate, and the course measured by a surveyor or qualified member of the Association." Today the time must be taken by three timekeepers, and where electrical timing is in operation, this is the time which will be recognised. In 1896 competitors had to wear "complete clothing from the shoulders to the knees, e.g. sleeved jersey and loose drawers". A sprinter who "beat the pistol" was penalised one yard for a first offence, two more yards if he repeated the fault, and if he faulted a third time he was disqualified. For similar offences a miler lost five yards. These rules were devised mainly for handicap events which were very much in vogue, but they also applied to scratch races.

Prizes for handicaps were limited to the value of ten guineas (a lot of money in those days), but in scratch events there appears to have been no limit. There were no lanes as we know them today. Instead, the course was marked by stakes at ten-yard intervals, each stake being linked by string. When I ran in the 1924 Olympics these stakes were still used.

As for performances, I give the world best — known for the years 1896 and 1971. World records were not officially recognised until after the foundation of the I.A.A.F. in 1912.

Metres	1896		1971	
	min.	sec.	min.	sec.
100		10·7		9·9
200		21·1		19·8
400		48·2		43·8
800	1	52·7	1	44·3
1,500	3	57·6	3	33·1
5,000	14	52·0	13	16·6
10,000	31	17·8	27	39·4
110 hurdles		15·2		13·2
400 hurdles		56·9		48·1

	metres	ft.	in.	metres	ft.	in.
High jump	1·97	6	5½	2·29	7	6¼
Pole vault	3·49	11	5½	5·49	18	0
Long jump	7·21	23	8	8·90	29	2½
Triple jump	14·78	48	6	17·40	57	1
Shot	14·33	47	0	21·78	71	5½
Discus	34·04	111	8	68·40	224	5
Hammer	44·46	145	10½	76·40	250	8
Javelin	44·00	144	4	92·70	304	1

There is no single reason for the fantastic improvement in athletic achievement. Conditions under which competitions are held have been much improved particularly in recent years with the many "all-weather" tracks, regarded now as essential for any top-class competition. Starting-blocks have made starting much easier and faster, though by how much is debatable.

Of course, in some events there has been a fundamental change in technique. The pole vault has been revolutionised by the use, first of a steel pole, and, since the early 1960s, of a fibreglass one. The "Fosbury Flop" would certainly have been ruled out up to the second world war, as would other styles. Again, the amount of training carried out by the modern athlete bears no relation to what was done even in my day — the early 1920s. Athletes now spend hours where we spent minutes.

However, the biggest factor must be the actual number of athletes involved. It is impossible to say how many hundreds of thousands of

Above: The starter and his assistant at the Tokyo Olympics

Below left: A modern running-shoe

Below right: Starting-blocks — another "aid" to modern sprinters

athletes there are today. Consequently, since 1960 the I.A.A.F. has been compelled to introduce qualifying standards for all events except the Marathon, the two walks and the relays. (A country can enter one competitor who has not reached the standard, but if it wishes to enter two or three — the latter being the maximum entry allowed — each must qualify.) Let me illustrate what this means. For the 1972 Games, the qualifying standard for the 1,500 metres is 3 min. 41·6 sec. — inside four minutes for the mile. Up until 1952, when Ron Delany won the gold medal in Melbourne in 3 min. 41·2 sec., no Olympic champion would have qualified for Munich. The time for the 5,000 metres (13 min. 48 sec.) is faster than Gunder Hägg, Emil Zatopek or Chris Chataway ever achieved. For the high jump you must now clear 7 ft. 0½ in. to be accepted. It was not until June 1956 that 7 ft. was cleared for the first time, and the first Olympic champion to exceed that height was the Russian Robert Shavlakadze in 1960.

In women's events the improvement has been equally impressive. When qualifying standards were first introduced in 1960, 2 min. 12·0 sec. was required for the 800 metres (this event was reintroduced in Rome after an interval of thirty-two years), 19 ft. 4¼ in. for the long jump and 47 ft. 10¼ in. for the shot. The 1972 standards for these three events are, respectively: 2 min. 5·0 sec., 20 ft. 8 in.; and 53 ft. 1¾ in. Last year (1971) thirty women beat the Olympic qualifying standard in the 800 metres, a similar number did 20 ft. 11 in. or better in the long jump, and thirty shot-putters reached 55 ft. Yet it is less than twenty years since the 800 metres world record was 2 min. 5 sec., that for the long jump under 21 ft., and for the shot under 54 ft.

Where will it all end? If I had been told in 1952 — just twenty years ago — that 1,500 metres would be run in 3 min. 33·1 sec. (the record was then 3 min. 43 sec., and the four-minute mile still unaccomplished); that 5,000 metres would be run in less than two seconds outside 13 min. 15 sec. (the record was then 13 min. 58·2 sec.); the shot putt reach within half an inch of 71 ft. 6 in. (compared with just short of 59 ft.), I might well have said, "Oh yes, and I suppose someone will reach the Moon too!" But it has all happened. And who is to say that in another twenty years we may not see 1,500 metres in 3 min. 30 sec., and so on? Of course, there must be a limit, and one is tempted to say that, however intense the training and perfect the techniques, that limit has nearly been reached. We must wait and see.

One of the most fascinating inventions since the second world war, so far as judging and timekeeping is concerned, is the photo-finish camera. This provides a photograph which shows the exact moment, to one-hundredth of a second, when each competitor reached the finish line. Look at the picture above of the 400 metres hurdles in Mexico. At the bottom you will see, reading from left to right, the figures 49·0 . . . 48·8 down to 48·0, with twenty divisions between each figure. The piece of film opposite 49·0 was exposed that number of seconds, and one-hundredths of a second, after the pistol starting the race was fired. Note that David Hemery's left foot reached

Sheila Sherwood and David Hemery outside Buckingham Palace after receiving their awards as "Athletes of the Year 1964" from H.R.H. Prince Philip, President of the British Amateur Athletic Board

the finish line in 48·0 sec., and his torso, which is what counts, in 48·08 sec. This is returned officially as 48·1 sec., since timing is to one-tenth of a second and not one-hundredth of a second for record purposes.

Now look along the picture to the left. The space between the winner and the other runners is not the distance by which Hemery won, but indicates the time which elapsed between Hemery reaching the line and the arrival of the others. The race between the second, third and fourth hurdlers was so close that I doubt if human judges could have come to an accurate decision. In fact, the second man was Gerhard Hennige of Germany in the inside lane, the third, John Sherwood of Great Britain in the outside lane, while Geoff Vanderstock of the U.S.A. in lane 3 was fourth, and the Russian Slava Skomorokov in lane 5 was fifth. It was a matter of inches between the four.

While the photo-finish has made "dead-heats" a rarity — though I have seen photo-finish pictures where it was still quite impossible to determine the winner — it has brought into sharp relief the exaggerated importance that is almost always attached to gold medallists. In particular, I recall the 400 metres in Mexico where Lillian Board was beaten by seven-hundredths of a second, which represented the difference between 100 per cent and 99·87 per cent. Alas, the winner gets all the glory, while the runner-up — on the day the second best in the whole world — is almost forgotten. To get into a national team at all, bearing in mind the exceptionally high standards required for entry, itself represents a great performance. To reach the final eight is something that merits, not the highest praise — that is rightly reserved for the winner — but praise indeed.

Men's Track Events

Dorando Pietri, the man whose "failure" in the 1908 Marathon gained him immortal fame and a special gold cup from Queen Alexandra

A BRITISH FLYER. By TOM WEBSTER.

THE REST

AT 6'O'CLOCK LAST NIGHT H.M. ABRAHAMS WON THE WORLD'S 100 METRES RACE IN PARIS.

The cartoon of the author which appeared in the Evening News of July 8th, 1924, the day after he had won the 100 metres in the Paris Olympics

At Munich there will be six individual running events, two hurdle races, a steeplechase, a Marathon and two walks for men. This programme was standardised in 1928. Previously there had been many changes since 1896 when there were only four running events and a hurdles. Cross-country events were held in 1912, 1920 and 1924. Relay running was first introduced in 1908, with a medley race over 200, 200, 400 and 800 metres stages. In 1912 this event was changed to 4×400 metres and a 4×100 metres event added.

The improvement in performance, especially over the last twenty years, has been phenomenal, as the following table of Olympic records shows:

Metres	1936		1952		1968	
	min.	sec.	min.	sec.	min.	sec.
100		10·3*		10·3		9·9
200		20·7		20·7		19·8
400		46·2		45·9		43·8
800	1	49·7 (1932)	1	49·2 (also 1948)	1	44·3
1,500	3	47·8	3	45·1	3	34·9
5,000	14	22·2	14	06·6	13	39·6 (1956)
10,000	30	11·4 (1932)	29	17·0	28	24·4 (1964)
Steeplechase	9	03·8	8	45·4	8	30·8 (1964)
110 hurdles		14·2		13·7		13·3
400 hurdles		52·0		50·8		48·1

The figures in parenthesis indicate where the record was broken in a previous year.

* This time was accomplished in 1932 and 1936. Jesse Owens did 10·2 sec. in 1936, but with too favourable a following wind.

During the whole history of the Games from 1896 to 1968, so far as track events are concerned, the following athletes won their events on more than one occasion:

The Jury of Appeal examine videotape to decide a "protest". The Marquis of Exeter (President of the I.A.A.F.) is on the left

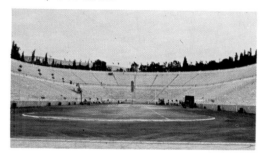

The marble stadium in Athens, built for the first modern Games in 1896

Mexico City — the Japanese hand over the Olympic Flag to the Mexicans, who will repeat the courtesy with the Germans next August

Hundreds of television sets for journalists at the closing ceremony of the Tokyo Olympics

800 metres: Douglas Lowe (1924 and 1928), Mal Whitfield (1948 and 1952), Peter Snell (1960 and 1964).

10,000 metres: Paavo Nurmi (1920 and 1928), Emil Zatopek (1948 and 1952)

Marathon: Abebe Bikila (1960 and 1964)

20,000 metres walk: Vladimir Golubnichy (1960 and 1968)

110 metres hurdles: Lee Calhoun (1956 and 1960)

400 metres hurdles: Glenn Davis (1956 and 1960)

In terms of individual performances, I have been present at ten of the eleven Olympics since 1920 and retain some outstanding memories of each:

1920 Antwerp
There was the sprinting of Charley Paddock with his famous "leap" at the finish. Also the first appearance of Paavo Nurmi — a defeat by Joseph Guillemot of France in the 5,000 metres, and his revenge three days later in the 10,000 metres.

1924 Paris
Eric Liddell's magnificent 400 metres (the last British gold medallist in this event) and Douglas Lowe's narrow victory in the 800 metres. Best of all, Paavo Nurmi's four wins — 1,500 and 5,000 metres on the same afternoon, followed by wins in the 3,000 metres team race and the cross-country.

1928 Amsterdam
Douglas Lowe's repeat victory in the 800 metres. There was also Lord Burghley's (now the Marquis of Exeter) fine win in the 400 metres hurdles, and Nurmi's ninth gold medal.

1932 Los Angeles
I missed these Games, in which we had the first victories of a coloured athlete in the sprints, and a world record victory by Tommy Hampson (Britain) in the 800 metres.

1936 Berlin
Jesse Owens, my ideal sprinter, supreme with victories in the 100 and 200 metres. Also Jack Lovelock with his new world record in the 1,500 metres.

1948 London
The first appearance of Emil Zatopek, who won the 10,000 metres by over three-quarters of a minute and beat the half-hour.

1952 Helsinki
Zatopek again, with a unique triple victory in the 5,000 and 10,000 metres and the Marathon, each with new Olympic best performances. There was also the desperate battle between the Jamaicans George Rhoden and Herb McKenley in the 400 metres, both given the same time of 45·9 sec., with Rhoden the winner.

1956 Melbourne
The Russian Vladimir Kuts's dual success in the 5,000 and 10,000 metres, and American Bobby Morrow's triple crown in the sprints and relay. Also Ron Delany's win for Eire in the 1,500 metres, in which the first nine beat the previous Olympic record, and Chris Brasher's win for Britain in the steeplechase.

1960 Rome
The first European victory in the 100 metres for thirty-six years by Armin Hary, and the first and only European victory in the 200 metres by Livio Berruti. Another astonishing victory which only the photo-finish camera could decide for the American Otis Davis in the 400 metres, while Herb Elliott gained a twenty-yard victory in the 1,500 metres in a new world record time, and the Ethiopian Abebe Bikila won the Marathon.

1964 Tokyo
A double for Peter Snell of New Zealand in the 800 and 1,500 metres. Abebe Bikila won his second Marathon in a time which averaged nearly 12 m.p.h. for the 26 miles.

1968 Mexico City
Another Ethiopian, Mamo Wolde, lost the gold medal in the 10,000 metres by less than a second, then won the Marathon by over three minutes. And there was David Hemery's world record victory for Britain in the 400 metres hurdles in 48·1 sec. — probably the greatest track performance of the Games.

100 Metres

It is more than one hundred years since a runner first recorded what was described as "even time" for 100 yards, the distance accepted as the shortest for championship events, and comparable to the 100 metres which has always been the race on the Continent and in the Olympic Games. "Even time" means running the distance at an average speed of ten yards a second, or 20·8 m.p.h.

The world records for 100 yards (9·1 sec.) and 100 metres — that is 109·3 yards (9·9 sec.) give an average speed of 22·5 m.p.h. It takes about fifty or sixty yards to achieve a maximum speed of very nearly 27 m.p.h., and so lavish is the expenditure of oxygen, which is the "fuel" of a runner, that this maximum speed can only be maintained for fifteen or twenty yards.

It was in 1890 that ten seconds was first breached over 100 yards, by the American John Owen. Twelve years later, another American, Arthur Duffey, gave us 9·6 sec. Almost another quarter of a century followed before Charley Paddock did 9·5 sec. This was not accepted by the International Federation as 9·5 sec., but as 9·6 sec., because it was not until 1929 that it was decided to recognise sprint records timed to one-tenth of a second. It is only right to mention that modern electrical timing, which can time to one-hundredth of a second — in which time a sprinter moves about four inches — has shown how unreliable human timing is. There must be a delay between the time when the time-keeper sees the flash of the pistol and starts his watch. Additionally, he is apt to anticipate the moment when the runner reaches the finish. These errors can amount to as much as one-fifth of a second.

In 1935, the coloured American, Jesse Owens, one of the greatest athletes of all time, did 9·4 sec. Thirteen years were to pass before the time was reduced to 9·3 sec., and another thirteen before 9·2 sec. was recorded.

In June 1963, Bob Hayes of the U.S.A. — the 1964 Olympic 100 metres champion — became the first man to clock 9·1 sec., and since then four other athletes have equalled this time. Undoubtedly 9·0 sec. will one day be achieved.

Over 100 metres, ten seconds was broken

Above: Armin Hary (Ger) — the first European to win the 100 metres for thirty-six years — beats David Sime (USA) in Rome, with Peter Radford (GB) third

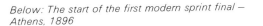

Below: The start of the first modern sprint final — Athens, 1896

Above: Don Quarrie (Jam), triple gold medallist in Edinburgh, wins the 100 metres from fellow-Jamaican Lennox Miller in 10·2 sec.

for the first time in June 1968 at Sacramento, U.S.A., when it was accomplished by three coloured Americans on the same afternoon.

Many are the arguments as to who is the greatest sprinter of all time. This is, of course, a matter of opinion, or perhaps it would be more accurate to say ''personal prejudice'', for it is quite impossible to compare the performance of one generation of performers with those of another. If I had to plump for one man, it would be Jesse Owens. On times Owens would be beaten today by three yards over 100 metres, but I believe that if it were possible to line up those who could claim to be considered the world's greatest, Jesse Owens should win. No sprinter I have ever seen was such a delight to watch.

Above: The fastest men in the world — Lennox Miller (Jam), Jim Hines (USA) and Charlie Greene (USA) on the victory stand in Mexico

Top: A clear win for Jim Hines (USA) in the 100 metres in Mexico, equalling the world record of 9·9 sec., with joint world record-holder Charlie Greene (third), nine inches behind Lennox Miller (Jam)

Charlie Greene (USA), one of the three men to beat 10·0 sec. for the 100 metres

100 METRES · OLYMPIC CHAMPIONS

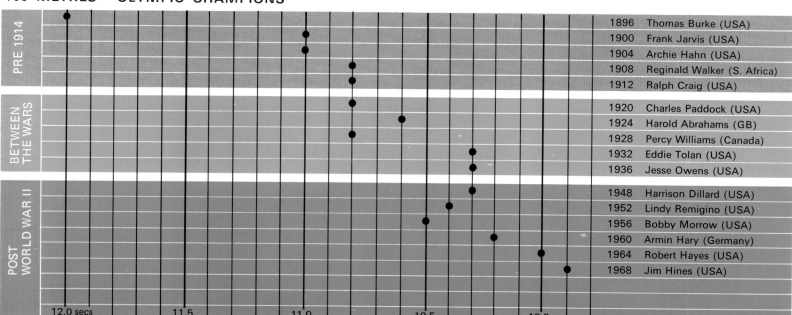

PRE 1914		1896	Thomas Burke (USA)
		1900	Frank Jarvis (USA)
		1904	Archie Hahn (USA)
		1908	Reginald Walker (S. Africa)
		1912	Ralph Craig (USA)
BETWEEN THE WARS		1920	Charles Paddock (USA)
		1924	Harold Abrahams (GB)
		1928	Percy Williams (Canada)
		1932	Eddie Tolan (USA)
		1936	Jesse Owens (USA)
POST WORLD WAR II		1948	Harrison Dillard (USA)
		1952	Lindy Remigino (USA)
		1956	Bobby Morrow (USA)
		1960	Armin Hary (Germany)
		1964	Robert Hayes (USA)
		1968	Jim Hines (USA)

12.0 secs   11.5   11.0   10.5   10.0

15

200 Metres

The 200 metres race, and its imperial distance of 220 yards — slightly less than two yards further — has never been anything like as popular as the 100 metres. In the United States, the 200 metres was introduced into the championship programme as early as 1877, but the British held no championship over 220 yards until 1902. The 200 metres race was not included in the first revived Olympic Games of 1896, but was staged four years later.

As early as September 1896, the American Bernie Wefers — regarded by some as the best sprinter of the nineteenth century — ran 200 metres over a straight course in 21·2 sec., and although this time was equalled on five occasions before the first world war, it was not until the advent of the American Charley Paddock, in 1921, that twenty-one seconds was beaten.

One of the athletes who had clocked 21·2 sec., in July 1914, was the Englishman, Willie Applegarth, possibly Britain's finest sprinter ever. Applegarth won his third British 220 yards title, run at the Stamford Bridge home of the Chelsea Football Club in 1914, round two bends in 21·2 sec. Two years earlier, he had finished third in the Olympic 200 metres final.

Like every event, the performance over 200 metres improved considerably between the wars. Jesse Owens did 20·3 sec. in May 1935, and it was fourteen years before this record was eclipsed.

In 1965, Tommie Smith ran the distance in 20·0 sec., and accomplished the astonishing time of 19·5 sec. over a straight course the following year. In winning the Olympic title in 1968, Smith did 19·8 sec. around a curve, just ahead of Peter Norman of Australia, the Commonwealth record-holder at that time.

Over the straight course, there have been thirteen United States world record-holders, and the only other runner to gain inclusion in this distinguished list is Willie Applegarth.

Round a turn, there have been eight United States world record-holders, a German, the Italian Olympic Champion, Livio Berruti, and the Englishman Peter Radford. Radford's time was done over 220 yards.

In the Olympic Games, the winner of the 100 metres has also won the 200 on six occasions, the last being in Australia in 1956, when Bobby Morrow of the U.S.A. was dual champion.

In 1908 and 1928, Canadians broke the American run of Olympic successes, but the first European to win the title was the Italian Livio Berruti in 1960. Before an Italian crowd, Berruti twice equalled the world record of 20·5 sec., and the cheering and stamping was such that the "official" photo-finish camera was nearly shaken from its tripod.

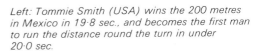

Left: Tommie Smith (USA) wins the 200 metres in Mexico in 19·8 sec., and becomes the first man to run the distance round the turn in under 20·0 sec.

Below: Willie Applegarth — British Olympic bronze medallist at Stockholm — equalling the world 220 yards record of 21·2 sec. at Stamford Bridge in July 1914. Applegarth was a member of the victorious British sprint relay team at Stockholm. Vic d'Arcy, another member of the team, is seen behind him

Above: Henry Carr (USA), world record-holder for the 200 metres and 220 yards (20·2 sec.) round the turn, and winner of the Olympic 200 metres in 1964 (20·3 sec.). Carr also anchored the victorious American 4×400 metres relay team in the world record time of 3 min. 0·7 sec.

Top right: Valeriy Borzov (USSR), dual European sprint champion, 1971, and a challenge to American sprinters at Munich

Don Quarrie (Jam) wins his second-round heat of the 200 metres in Edinburgh in 20·4 sec. — the fastest ever on a British track, but with a following wind of over 10 m.p.h.

Livio Berruti (Italy), the only European to win the Olympic 200 metres, delighted the Italian crowd with his 1960 victory in the Olympic record time of 20·5 sec.

200 METRES · OLYMPIC CHAMPIONS

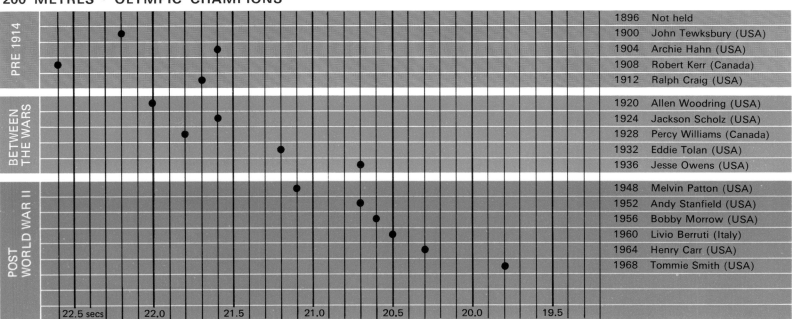

	1896	Not held
	1900	John Tewksbury (USA)
PRE 1914	1904	Archie Hahn (USA)
	1908	Robert Kerr (Canada)
	1912	Ralph Craig (USA)
	1920	Allen Woodring (USA)
	1924	Jackson Scholz (USA)
BETWEEN THE WARS	1928	Percy Williams (Canada)
	1932	Eddie Tolan (USA)
	1936	Jesse Owens (USA)
	1948	Melvin Patton (USA)
	1952	Andy Stanfield (USA)
POST WORLD WAR II	1956	Bobby Morrow (USA)
	1960	Livio Berruti (Italy)
	1964	Henry Carr (USA)
	1968	Tommie Smith (USA)

22.5 secs   22.0   21.5   21.0   20.5   20.0   19.5

400 Metres

Four hundred metres is just about eight feet short of the 440 yards, and is now one lap of all standard tracks. The race, which in the early days was regarded as a middle-distance event, has now become a controlled sprint, since the world record of 43·8 sec., set up in the Mexican Olympics in 1968, does represent what the old sprinters called "even time" — that is to say, an average speed of ten yards a second.

So far as the Olympic Games is concerned, the United States have won the gold medal eleven times, Great Britain and Jamaica on two occasions each, and South Africa once. Bevil Rudd, who won the 400 metres for South Africa in 1920, was actually born in Cornwall.

Great Britain's two victories, both by Scotsmen, are remembered for particular reasons.

In 1908, the records show that the winner "walked over". He was Captain Wyndham Halswelle, a great Scottish athlete who once won four Scottish championships in one afternoon. In the Olympic final he was opposed by three Americans, one of whom was disqualified for "obstruction", and the race was ordered to be rerun. But the two

Below: Lee Evans (USA) wins the 1968 Olympic 400 metres in the world record time of 43·8 sec., becoming the first man to run the distance at an average speed of under 11 sec. per 100 metres

Americans, who were entitled to take part in the rerun race, declined to do so, and Halswelle ran over on his own in 50·0 sec. Halswelle had already run 48·4 sec. for a new Olympic record in his heat.

Until this time, the race had not been run in lanes, but after 1908 lanes were introduced and became obligatory. This meant the runners started in "echelon", so that each covered the right distance.

Great Britain's second win, in 1924, was through Eric Liddell. Liddell was the son of a Scottish missionary, and a deeply religious man. In 1923, he had won the British 100 and 220 yards championships, but when he discovered that the two first rounds of the 100 metres in the 1924 Paris Olympics were

Above: Archie Williams (USA) just beats Godfrey Brown (GB) in the 1936 Olympic 400 metres final

Below: Two Jamaicans share the Olympic record of 45·9 sec., but George Rhoden snatches the "gold" from Herb McKenley at Helsinki

Below: Robbie Brightwell (GB), fourth in the Tokyo 400 metres, in which race he equalled the United Kingdom record of 45·7 sec.

to be run on a Sunday, he said he would not compete and turned his attention to the 400 metres. Running with almost fanatical determination, he won the 400 metres in the new Olympic record time of 47·6 sec.

In the role of world record-holders, there have been fourteen Americans, two Germans and two Jamaicans. The two Germans were Rudolf Harbig who, three weeks before the outbreak of the second world war, did 46·0 sec. which remained a record for nearly nine years, and Carl Kaufmann. The Jamaicans were Herbert McKenley, twice an Olympic silver medallist, and George Rhoden. Rhoden beat McKenley by inches in the 1952 Olympics, but they shared the Olympic record with 45·9 sec.

Charles Asati of Kenya, a clear winner of the 1970 Commonwealth 400 metres in 45·0 sec. — a United Kingdom All-comers' record

David Jenkins (GB), who missed the Commonwealth Games in Edinburgh, but won the European title in 1971 in 45·5 sec., a new United Kingdom record. Still only twenty years old, David has a real chance of a medal in Munich

400 METRES · OLYMPIC CHAMPIONS

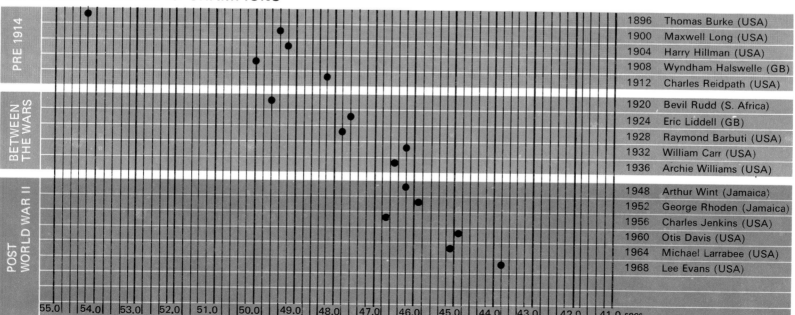

PRE 1914	1896	Thomas Burke (USA)
	1900	Maxwell Long (USA)
	1904	Harry Hillman (USA)
	1908	Wyndham Halswelle (GB)
	1912	Charles Reidpath (USA)
BETWEEN THE WARS	1920	Bevil Rudd (S. Africa)
	1924	Eric Liddell (GB)
	1928	Raymond Barbuti (USA)
	1932	William Carr (USA)
	1936	Archie Williams (USA)
POST WORLD WAR II	1948	Arthur Wint (Jamaica)
	1952	George Rhoden (Jamaica)
	1956	Charles Jenkins (USA)
	1960	Otis Davis (USA)
	1964	Michael Larrabee (USA)
	1968	Lee Evans (USA)

55.0 | 54.0 | 53.0 | 52.0 | 51.0 | 50.0 | 49.0 | 48.0 | 47.0 | 46.0 | 45.0 | 44.0 | 43.0 | 42.0 | 41.0 secs

800 Metres

The 800 metres was one of the events at the very first of the modern Olympic meetings in 1896, when it was won by an Australian, Edwin Flack, in a time of 2 min. 11·0 sec. Its equivalent event in Britain of 880 yards, was one of the events in the British Amateur Championships when they started in 1866. At one time, perhaps even up to the second world war, the distance was regarded as a middle-distance event, but since the second world war, it has been regarded almost as a sprint.

As in other athletic events, there has been a gradual improvement in performances. Two minutes for 880 yards was first beaten in 1873, and it was another fifteen years before Englishman Frank Cross beat 1 min. 55·0 sec.

Forty-four years passed, and another Englishman, Tommy Hampson, got inside 1 min. 50·0 sec. over 800 metres and gave Great Britain an Olympic gold medal. It was the fourth Olympics in succession that this event had been won by a Great Britain representative.

Then, in August 1938, Britain's Sydney Wooderson set up a new world record of 1 min. 48·4 sec., and less than eleven months later Rudolf Harbig of Germany, the European champion, created a sensation when he ran 800 metres in 1 min. 46·6 sec. This record was to stand for sixteen years.

By the end of 1971, over sixty athletes had run 800 metres in 1 min. 46·6 sec. — all of them since 1955.

One and three-quarter minutes was first beaten in 1962, by the 1960 Olympic champion Peter Snell, in the present (1971) world record time of 1 min. 44·3 sec. This was equalled by Ralph Doubell of Australia when winning the 1968 Olympic gold medal. Jim Ryun's time of 1 min. 44·9 sec. for 880 yards is just slightly better as a performance.

In the Olympic Games, the 800 metres title has always been won by an American athlete, or one from the British Commonwealth. Five athletes have won both the 800 and 1,500 metres gold medals. Two of these were Americans — Lightbody in 1904 and Sheppard in 1908. Edwin Flack, from Australia, did the double in 1896, Albert Hill from Great Britain triumphed in 1920, and finally Peter Snell from New Zealand won both gold medals in 1964.

Douglas Lowe (1924 and 1928), Mal Whitfield (1948 and 1952) and Peter Snell (1960 and 1964) are the three Olympic champions who have successfully defended their 800 metres titles. The most remarkable of the three was Peter Snell. An "outsider" at the 1960 Games in Rome, he moved almost three seconds faster than he had run before, to beat Roger Moens of Belgium, and the previous Olympic record, by 1·4 sec. Four years later, having in the meantime set up world records for both the 800 metres and one mile, Snell successfully defended his 800 metres Games title and beat his own Olympic record by 1·2 sec. Five days later, he completed the brilliant double with a win in the 1,500 metres.

In the Olympics, four countries have provided gold medallists — the United States claiming seven medals and Great Britain five — her most successful event in the Games.

Below: Peter Snell (NZ) wins his first Olympic 800 metres title in Rome, beating world record-holder Roger Moens (Bel) in the new Olympic record time of 1 min. 46·3 sec. Snell later set up a new world record of 1 min. 44·3 sec.

Above: Mal Whitfield (USA) retains his Olympic 800 metres title in Helsinki in 1 min. 49·2 sec., equalling the Olympic record he established four years earlier

Left: Yevgeniy Arzhanov (USSR) winning the European 800 metres championship in 1971 in 1 min. 45·5 sec. Above: Recovering after the race

Above: Douglas Lowe (GB), the first man ever to retain an Olympic track title. Lowe won the 800 metres in Paris in 1 min. 52·4 sec., and in Amsterdam set up a new Olympic record of 1 min. 51·8 sec.

Top: Ralph Doubell (Aus) has to equal the world record of 1 min. 44·3 sec. to snatch the 1968 Olympic title from Wilson Kirprugut of Kenya. Thus for the third Games in succession an Australasian won the event

Above: Robert Ouko (Ken) leads Bill Smart (Can) and Chris Fisher (Aus) in the 800 metres Commonwealth final, which he won in 1 min. 46·8 sec.

800 METRES · OLYMPIC CHAMPIONS

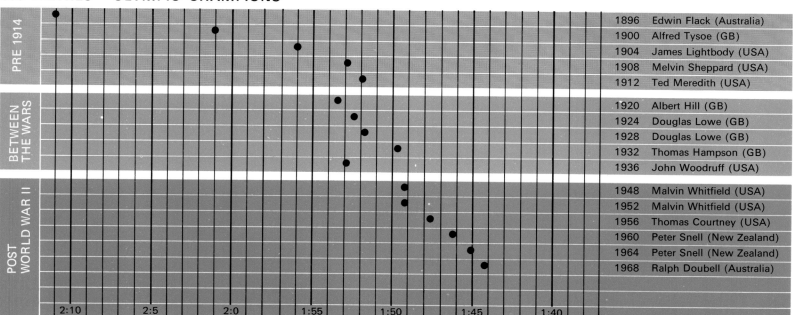

PRE 1914	1896	Edwin Flack (Australia)
	1900	Alfred Tysoe (GB)
	1904	James Lightbody (USA)
	1908	Melvin Sheppard (USA)
	1912	Ted Meredith (USA)
BETWEEN THE WARS	1920	Albert Hill (GB)
	1924	Douglas Lowe (GB)
	1928	Douglas Lowe (GB)
	1932	Thomas Hampson (GB)
	1936	John Woodruff (USA)
POST WORLD WAR II	1948	Malvin Whitfield (USA)
	1952	Malvin Whitfield (USA)
	1956	Thomas Courtney (USA)
	1960	Peter Snell (New Zealand)
	1964	Peter Snell (New Zealand)
	1968	Ralph Doubell (Australia)

2:10   2:5   2:0   1:55   1:50   1:45   1:40

1,500 Metres

It seems curious that there should be a race over 1,500 metres. The reason is possibly that most tracks abroad, in the latter part of the last century, were 500 metres in circumference, and races were held over two, three or four laps, and so on. To get the nearest approach to the mile, the race would have to be 1,600 metres, which is exactly four laps of the modern 400-metre circuit.

One day, I feel sure we shall change the 1,500 metres to a race of 1,600 metres, which would be a "metric mile" and only 12 yards short of the imperial one.

The Olympic 1,500 metres has seen gold medals distributed far and wide among different countries. Great Britain claims three victories — in 1900, 1912 and 1920; the United States, Australia, Finland and New Zealand, two each, while Eire, Italy, Luxembourg, Kenya and Sweden each have one race to their credit. Great Britain has not won this event since 1920, while the United States' last victory was in 1908.

The 1,500 metres has produced some of the most exciting and interesting races of all events. In 1924, the great Paavo Nurmi led from start to finish, beating the Olympic record by over three seconds, and just one second slower than the world record he himself had made only three weeks before. Finland was again successful in 1928, while at Los Angeles in 1932, Italian Luigi Beccali strode away to beat the Olympic record-

holder, Larva of Finland. Larva finished eighth, and Jack Lovelock of New Zealand was just behind him.

In the 1936 Berlin final, four years later, Beccali successfully defended his title against six of the twelve finalists who had competed in the Los Angeles final. Since 1932, Lovelock had reduced the one mile record to 4 min. 7.6 sec., and within a year American Glenn Cunningham had removed four-fifths of a second from Lovelock's time. It was thought by many that Cunningham and Beccali would fight out the 1936 Olympic finish, with the American determined to have his revenge for his 1932 defeat. In the event, however, Jack Lovelock ran an inspired race and judged his final winning sprint to perfection, to take more

than three seconds off the existing Olympic record and one second off the world best. Cunningham, five yards behind, beat Beccali by about the same margin for second place.

It was twenty-four years before another Australasian, Herb Elliot, emulated Lovelock's feat — namely, an Olympic gold medal and a world record in the same race. Elliott's time of 3 min. 35.6 sec. beat the previous Olympic record by over five seconds, and his own world record by four-tenths of a second.

It was the brilliant Kenyan runner, Kipchoge Keino, who overcame the problems of height in Mexico, in 1968 to win in 3 min. 34.9 sec.

Over a period of forty years, the Olympic record had been reduced by over 18 seconds, which is over 120 yards faster running.

Above: Francesco Arese (Italy) leads in the 1971 European 1,500 metres final, which he won in 3 min. 38.4 sec.

Below: A surprise victory for Luxembourg's Josef Barthel in the 1952 Olympic 1,500 metres, which he won from Robert McMillen (USA) in 3 min. 45.2 sec.

Above: New Zealand's Jack Lovelock (No. 467) winning the great 1,500 metres final in Berlin in the world record time of 3 min. 47.8 sec. Times have certainly changed — the qualifying time for Munich is 3 min. 41.8 sec.

Above: Herb Elliott (Aus) wins the Olympic 1,500 metres in Rome by nearly three seconds in the new world record time of 3 min. 35.6 sec.

Right: Kip Keino (Ken) leads Dick Quax (NZ) in the final of the 1970 Commonwealth 1,500 metres, which Keino won in 3 min. 36·6 sec.

Below: Jim Ryun (USA), second to Keino in the Mexican Olympics 1,500 metres, but still world record-holder for the 880 yards, 1,500 metres and one mile

1,500 METRES · OLYMPIC CHAMPIONS

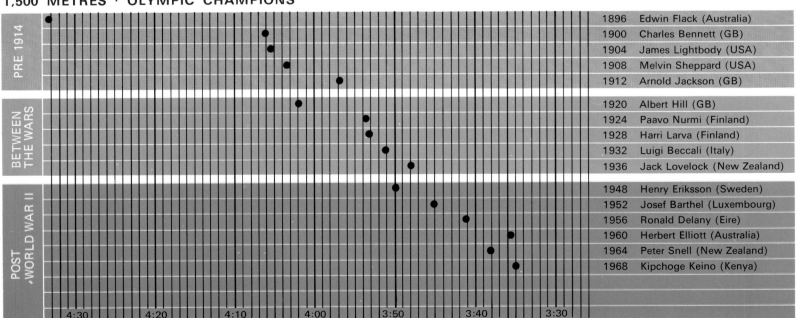

PRE 1914	1896	Edwin Flack (Australia)
	1900	Charles Bennett (GB)
	1904	James Lightbody (USA)
	1908	Melvin Sheppard (USA)
	1912	Arnold Jackson (GB)
BETWEEN THE WARS	1920	Albert Hill (GB)
	1924	Paavo Nurmi (Finland)
	1928	Harri Larva (Finland)
	1932	Luigi Beccali (Italy)
	1936	Jack Lovelock (New Zealand)
POST WORLD WAR II	1948	Henry Eriksson (Sweden)
	1952	Josef Barthel (Luxembourg)
	1956	Ronald Delany (Eire)
	1960	Herbert Elliott (Australia)
	1964	Peter Snell (New Zealand)
	1968	Kipchoge Keino (Kenya)

4:30 4:20 4:10 4:00 3:50 3:40 3:30

The Mile

The "mile" owes its origin to the Latin *mille*, which means a thousand. It was a unit of measurement of one thousand paces, calculated to be something over 1,600 yards. How the English mile came to be 1,760 yards is a bit of a mystery, and miles in some other countries are of different lengths. But be that as it may, it has always been a popular distance, even abroad where the metric system has been in vogue for nearly two centuries.

Though the "four-minute" mile is an achievement that caught the public imagination almost more than any other happening in athletic history, it was not until the 1940s that people regarded this as a possibility. But more than half a century before, the mile was regarded as "the event" of any athletic meet-ing, and there are apocryphal stories of "running footmen" covering the distance on the road in four minutes. By 1870, two genuine amateur performers had achieved inside four and a half minutes, and by the end of the nineteenth century, amateurs were within three-fifths of a second of four and a quarter minutes. But a very great runner named Walter George, who as an amateur had won ten British championships from one to ten miles, and become the first man to beat 4 min. 20.0 sec for the mile as a professional in 1886, ran the distance in 4 min. 12¾ sec. At that date, stop-watches were graduated to quarter-seconds, not as now to one-fifth or one-tenth.

It was not until 1915 — almost thirty years later, that an amateur did 4 min. 12.6 sec. to eclipse George's record by the narrow margin of under one-fifth of a second. Another eight years and the Flying Finn, Paavo Nurmi, got within two-fifths of a second of 4 min. 10 sec., then eight more before a Frenchman did 4 min. 9.2 sec. By the outbreak of the second world war, Sydney Wooderson had re-captured the world mile record for Britain after forty-two years, with 4 min. 6.4 sec., and this remained the best for nearly five years.

Then, during the war, two Swedish milers, Gunder Hägg and Arne Andersson, eventually brought it down to 4 min. 1.3 sec. That is about ten yards slower than the fascinating four minutes.

In the 1950s, the serious assault on four minutes began. But it was not until May 6th, 1954, that Roger Bannister, at the age of twenty-five, was paced by Christopher Chataway and Christopher Brasher to break the four-minute barrier by three-fifths of a second.

It is worth recording that Chataway subsequently set up world records for 3 miles and 5,000 metres, while Brasher became Olympic steeplechase champion in 1956. However, it had taken nearly nine years to remove that 1.3 sec.

But, within six weeks, the Australian John Landy clocked a time of 3 min. 57.9 sec. to improve Bannister's time by a further one and a half seconds. By the end of 1963, over forty runners had beaten four minutes, and at the end of 1971, 139 athletes were eligible for the "Four Minute" Club. The world record was within 1.1 sec. of 3 min. 50.0 sec., and the public was apt to slow-handclap a race outside the four-minute mark.

Below: Two inside four minutes. Roger Bannister passes John Landy near the finish of the 1954 Commonwealth mile. Time — Bannister, 3 min. 58.8 sec.; Landy, 3 min. 59.6 sec.

Below: In August 1937, after an interval of forty-two years, the mile record returned to Britain, when Sydney Wooderson ran the distance in 4 min. 6.4 sec. Wooderson also gained world records in the 800 metres and 880 yards a year later

Above: Herb Elliott wins the mile at the 1958 Commonwealth Games, having previously won the 880 yards

Above: Kip Keino who set up the United Kingdom All-comers' mile record (3 min. 53·4 sec.) in August 1966

Just after 6 p.m. on May 6th, 1954 — the four-minute barrier broken at last. Chris Brasher leads Roger Bannister and Chris Chataway en route.

Below: One of the three watches on which the time — 3 min. 59·4 sec. — was recorded

THE MILE · WORLD RECORDS 1913 –1967

mins. secs.			country	date	place
4	14·4	John Paul Jones	USA	31. 5.1913	Cambridge, Mass.
4	12·6	Norman Taber	USA	16. 7.1915	Cambridge, Mass.
4	10·4	Paavo Nurmi	Finland	23. 8.1923	Stockholm
4	09·2	Jules Ladoumègue	France	4.10.1931	Paris
4	07·6	Jack Lovelock	New Zealand	15. 7.1933	Princeton, N.J.
4	06·8	Glenn Cunningham	USA	16. 6.1934	Princeton, N.J.
4	06·4	Sydney Wooderson	GB & NI	28. 8.1937	Motspur Park
4	06·2	Gunder Hägg	Sweden	1. 7.1942	Gothenburg
4	06·2	Arne Andersson	Sweden	10. 7.1942	Stockholm
4	04·6	Gunder Hägg	Sweden	4. 9.1942	Stockholm
4	02·6	Arne Andersson	Sweden	1. 7.1943	Gothenburg
4	01·6	Arne Andersson	Sweden	18. 7.1944	Malmö
4	01·4	Gunder Hägg	Sweden	17. 7.1945	Malmö
3	59·4	Roger Bannister	GB & NI	6. 5.1954	Oxford
3	58·0	John Landy	Australia	21. 6.1954	Turku, Finland
3	57·2	Derek Ibbotson	GB & NI	19. 7.1957	London
3	54·5	Herb Elliott	Australia	6. 8.1958	Dublin
3	54·4	Peter Snell	New Zealand	27. 1.1962	Wanganui
3	54·1	Peter Snell	New Zealand	17.11.1964	Auckland
3	53·6	Michel Jazy	France	9. 6.1965	Rennes
3	51·3	Jim Ryun	USA	17. 7.1966	Berkeley, Calif.
3	51·1	Jim Ryun	USA	23. 6.1967	Bakersfield, Calif.

5,000 Metres

The 5,000 metres, which is equivalent to three miles plus one hundred and eighty-eight yards, was not introduced into the Olympic Games until the Vth Modern Olympiad, held in Stockholm in 1912. That year the first of the "Flying Finns", Hannes Kolehmainen, won in the then new world record time of 14 min. 36·6 sec. For the next thirty years, Scandinavians dominated the world scene. The last Scandinavian to hold the world record, and incidentally the first man to beat fourteen minutes for the distance, was Gunder Hägg of Sweden. Since 1942, the world record has been gained by a Czech (Emil Zatopek), a Russian (Vladimir Kuts), two Englishmen (Christopher Chataway and Gordon Pirie), a Hungarian (Sandor Iharos) and, more recently, Kipchoge Keino from Kenya and Ron Clarke from Australia.

The world record of Gunder Hägg stood for twelve years, until Zatopek broke it by the very narrow margin of one second. But, in the next twelve years from 1954 to 1966, it was lowered by some forty seconds. Finally came 13 min. 16·6 sec., by Ron Clarke, and it seems probable that in the future someone will run the distance in under thirteen minutes.

Only in one Olympic race, the first, has the world record been beaten for, in the Games, athletes run to win and ignore the time. Indeed, the Olympic record at the start of the 1970s, set up by Vladimir Kuts in 1956, was twenty-three seconds slower than the existing world record.

The first two Olympic races produced Franco-Finnish duels. In 1912, Kolehmainen beat the French 10,000 metres world record-holder, Jean Bouin, by less than two yards. Eight years later, another Frenchman, Joseph Guillemot, took revenge over an inexperienced Paavo Nurmi by winning with nearly five seconds to spare. But four years later this same Nurmi, within little more than one hour after winning the Olympic 1,500 metres, beat another Finn, Ville Ritola, in the 5,000 metres. In both races, Nurmi set new Olympic records — that for the 5,000 metres was within three seconds of his own world record. At the next three Olympics we had Finnish victories.

After the second world war, Emil Zatopek and Vladimir Kuts became names with which to conjure. Zatopek held world records from 5,000 metres to 30,000. With his rolling style, and almost always agonised expression, he looked at his last gasp as he reeled off lap after lap. Kuts followed Zatopek's double victories in the 5,000 and 10,000 metres in 1952, with a similar feat in the 1956 Games.

Two Englishmen, Chataway and Pirie, ran famous races against these two. Chataway, a comparative novice at Helsinki, led the field half a lap from the finish over 5,000 metres, but fell exhausted at the last corner. Pirie, having beaten Kuts in a new world record time in June 1956, was pulverised by Kuts over 5,000 metres at Melbourne in December.

Chataway, beaten by Kuts in the European Championships in August 1954, ran a 5,000 metres race against him at the White City some six weeks later and won by a stride before a huge, delirious crowd. He had beaten Kuts's world record by five seconds.

But what can one say about Ron Clarke, who eventually removed no less than eighteen seconds from Kuts's world record? Clarke, a magnificent running machine, never won a major title either in the Olympic or Commonwealth Games.

Vladimir Kuts (USSR) ahead of Gordon Pirie (GB) and Derek Ibbotson (GB) in the 5,000 metres at Melbourne. Kuts's time (13 min. 39·6 sec.) is still the Olympic record

Mohamed Gammoudi (Tunisia) just beats the two Kenyans Kip Keino and Naftali Temu for the 1968 5,000 metres title. The time of 14 min. 0·5 sec. was "slow" because of altitude

Emil Zatopek (Cze) in the 5,000 metres at Helsinki, followed by Herbert Schade (Ger) and Chris Chataway (GB). Zatopek won three gold medals at the 1952 Games

Right: Ian Stewart (Scot), a brilliant winner of the 5,000 metres Commonwealth title in 1970 in the European record time of 13 min. 22·8 sec. He was less than a second ahead of fellow-Scot Ian McCafferty, with Kip Keino third

In the 5,000 metres in Mexico City, 1968 the altitude had its predicted effect on those who were not acclimatised. The Olympic medal-winners — Gammoudi of Tunisia, Keino and Temu of Kenya — had all lived at heights comparable with the 7,500 feet of Mexico City.

As with other events, the all-round standard of performance has shown amazing improvement. At the end of 1971, forty-five athletes had beaten 13 min. 35·0 sec., which was the world record up to 1965.

Juha Vaatainen of Finland (No. 738) set the Helsinki stadium alight with a fine victory in the 1971 European 5,000 metres event

Australia's Ron Clarke, holder of seventeen world records, but who never secured an Olympic or Commonwealth "gold". His world records for 5,000 metres (13 min. 16·6 sec.) and 10,000 metres (27 min. 39·4 sec.) still stand

5,000 METRES · OLYMPIC CHAMPIONS

PRE 1914	1896–1908 Not held
	1912 Hannes Kolehmainen (Finland)
BETWEEN THE WARS	1920 Joseph Guillemot (France)
	1924 Paavo Nurmi (Finland)
	1928 Ville Ritola (Finland)
	1932 Lauri Lehtinen (Finland)
	1936 Gunnar Höckert (Finland)
POST WORLD WAR II	1948 Gaston Reiff (Belgium)
	1952 Emil Zátopek (Czechoslovakia)
	1956 Vladimir Kuts (USSR)
	1960 Murray Halberg (New Zealand)
	1964 Robert Schul (USA)
	1968 Mohamed Gammoudi (Tunisia)

14:50 14:40 14:30 14:20 14:10 14:00 13:50 13:40 13:30

10,000 Metres

This event, which is twenty-five laps of a 400-metre track, and some sixty yards short of six and a quarter miles, was first introduced into the Olympic Games held in Stockholm in 1912. Although on that date there were only thirty competitors, three preliminary heats were held on one day, with the final on the next. The winner was Hannes Kolehmainen from Finland, and that same country provided the winners for the next three Games — Paavo Nurmi won in 1920, Ville Ritola in 1924, and Nurmi again in 1928. Ritola won in a new world record time, and this was the only occasion on which a world-best performance in this event was set up at the Games.

But, in 1928, Paavo Nurmi, who had previously won the Olympic title in Antwerp in 1920, beat Ritola's Games record by over four seconds, and Ritola himself by the narrow margin of six-tenths of a second. There was an even narrower margin eight years later in Berlin, when Finland had first three places and Ilmari Salminen won with only two-tenths of a second to spare. This was the last occasion upon which Finland had an Olympic medallist in this event.

Twelve years later, in London 1948, Emil Zatopek appeared as a comparative unknown, and gained the easiest of Olympic victories. He was over forty-seven seconds ahead of the second man, to beat thirty minutes for the first time ever in this event in the Games. Four years later Zatopek repeated his success, beating his own Olympic record by forty-two seconds. Indeed, the first six in this race beat Zatopek's old 1948 record. In the following Games the Olympic record continued to be bettered, first by Vladimir Kuts, then by fellow-Russian, Pyotyr Bolotnikov. Finally in Tokyo 1964, the United States gained her first-ever Olympic victory in this event when William Mills beat Mohamed Gammoudi of Tunisia by two-fifths of a second, with the world record-holder Ron Clarke of Australia in third place and another second behind.

In Mexico in 1968, the high altitude played havoc with Olympic times. A Kenyan, Naftali Temu, beat an Ethiopian, Mamo Wolde, by three-fifths of a second, with Gammoudi third. The time was more than a minute slower than the Olympic record, due entirely to the

Above: Lachie Stewart of Scotland gained a surprise win over Ron Clarke (Aus) in the 1970 Commonwealth 10,000 metres in 28 min. 11·8 sec.

Above: After twenty-five years, a Finn wins a major title. Juha Vaatainen leading European record-holders Dave Bedford (GB) and Jurgen Haase (GDR) in the 1971 10,000 metres European Championship

Below: Vladimir Kuts (USSR) leads Gordon Pirie (GB) in the 10,000 metres at Melbourne. Kuts gave the Soviet Union her first-ever Olympic gold medal on the track

rarity of the atmosphere. The first four men had all lived and trained at high altitude.

The first world record-holder was a Frenchman Jean Bouin, whose time was just inside thirty-one minutes, recorded in 1911. By 1924, Paavo Nurmi had reduced this world time to six seconds outside the half-hour — an average speed of under five minutes per mile.

Just after the outbreak of the second world war, another Finn, Taisto Maki, beat thirty minutes, and in August 1950 Emil Zatopek was only two and six-tenths of a second outside twenty-nine minutes. Four years later Zatopek did 28 min. 54·2 sec., and another decade was to pass before twenty-eight minutes was eclipsed. That was in July 1965, when the Australian Ron Clarke achieved the

fantastic time of 27 minutes 39·4 sec., which represents an average speed of four and a half minutes for each mile.

Then, in July 1971, Britain's David Bedford ran what was at the time, the second fastest 10,000 metres ever, in 27 min. 47 sec.

By the end of 1971, seven athletes had beaten 28 min., and more than fifty had run the distance in under 28 min. 30 sec.

Right: "The Flying Finn." Paavo Nurmi held every world record from 1,500 to 20,000 metres, and in three successive Olympics collected nine gold medals. He twice won the 10,000 metres — in 1920 and 1928

Naftali Temu (Ken) ahead of Ron Clarke (Aus) in the 10,000 metres at Mexico. Temu finished less than a second ahead of Mamo Wolde of Ethiopia, who subsequently won the Marathon

10,000 METRES · OLYMPIC CHAMPIONS

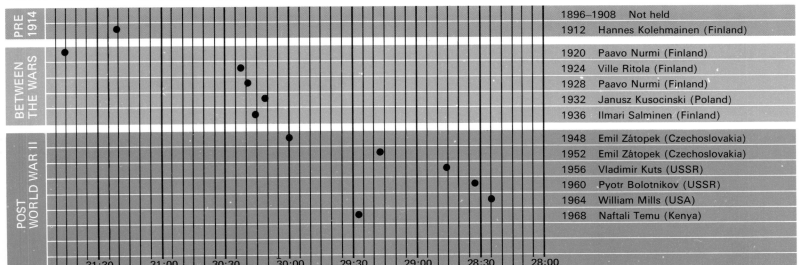

1896–1908	Not held
1912	Hannes Kolehmainen (Finland)
1920	Paavo Nurmi (Finland)
1924	Ville Ritola (Finland)
1928	Paavo Nurmi (Finland)
1932	Janusz Kusocinski (Poland)
1936	Ilmari Salminen (Finland)
1948	Emil Zátopek (Czechoslovakia)
1952	Emil Zátopek (Czechoslovakia)
1956	Vladimir Kuts (USSR)
1960	Pyotr Bolotnikov (USSR)
1964	William Mills (USA)
1968	Naftali Temu (Kenya)

The Marathon

Look up the word "marathon" in a dictionary, and you will find the following, or similar information: "This now familiar word for a long-distance race, and, by extension, for any other long-drawn-out test of endurance, was introduced in the first revived Olympic Games in Athens in 1896. The battle of Marathon, in which the Greeks defeated the invading Persians in 490 B.C. is said to have been marked by two notable long-distance runs. One, recorded by Herodotus, was that of a professional runner Phidippides, who ran one hundred and fifty miles from Athens to Sparta to request help for the impending battle. The other, not mentioned by Herodotus, was that of a soldier who ran 'in full armour, hot from the battle' (according to Plutarch) twenty-two miles to Athens to announce the victory, and fell dead from exhaustion as he did so. Plutarch says it was uncertain whether the name of the soldier was Thersippus or Eucles, but Lucian later attributed the exploit to Phidippides himself, a version popularised by Browning in his poem with that title."

Distance competitions, often over hundreds of miles, were commonplace for professionals in the last century. But there would, in all probability, never have been a long-distance event in the 1896 Olympics had not a Frenchman named Michel Breal, offered a special trophy for a race to be run from the plains of Marathon to the newly erected stadium in the city of Athens — a distance estimated at something just under twenty-five miles. The "traditional" distance for the Marathon is now 26 miles 385 yards, which happens to be the distance run in the 1908 Marathon race from Windsor to the Stadium at the White City.

The Marathon at the Olympics has produced many dramas, and the very first race in 1896 was good theatre. The Greek athletes had thoroughly disappointed their fellow-countrymen with not one victory in track and field, until the very last event, in which the Marathon was won by a Greek shepherd, Spyridon Louis, in just under three hours. Other Greeks were also second, fourth, fifth and sixth.

Four years later, it was run round the streets of Paris, on a very warm July day, and only seven out of nineteen competitors finished. The winner, Michel Theato, was said to have been a local baker's roundsman, and familiar with many short cuts. However, he won from a fellow Frenchman, Emile Champion, in fifteen seconds under three hours over a distance which was 25 miles.

The truly epic race took place in 1908, when an Italian, Dorando Pietri, entered the stadium well ahead of the rest of the Olympic field, only to collapse on the track. He was almost literally dragged over the finish by enthusiastic officials and compatriots, but was sadly and inevitably disqualified. But for this incident, before an 80,000 crowd, no one would ever have heard of Pietri, just as practically no one can tell you who won. It was American John Hayes.

At over thirty years of age, the great Hannes Kolehmainen won the 1920 Olympic Marathon in Antwerp, the first over an out-and-home course, which is now compulsory.

The 1928 victor was an Arab representing France, El Oufai, and an Argentinian named Juan Zabala, beat Sam Ferris of Great Britain by nineteen seconds at Los Angeles four years later. Another British athlete, Ernest Harper, was second to a Japanese, Kitei Son, in Berlin

in 1936, when two and a half hours was beaten for the first time. Twelve years later a third Great Britain representative, the Welshman Tommy Richards, won a silver medal, finishing sixteen seconds behind Delfo Cabrera of Argentine.

Britain's fourth silver medal came in 1964 through Basil Heatley, when the winner was Abebe Bikila, of Ethiopia. Bikila, having won in Rome in 1960, became the first man to retain the title.

Above: A surprise win for Belgium. At Helsinki Karel Lismont sets up a new European championship record of 2 hr. 13 min. 9 sec.

Below: Emil Zatopek (Cze) enters the Helsinki stadium to win the Marathon by over two and a half minutes

Below: The honour of Greece is saved. Spyridon Louis wins the first-ever Marathon — the only Greek victory in the 1896 Games

Top left: Ron Hill of England wins the 1970 Commonwealth title in 2 hr. 9 min. 28 sec.

Above left: Mamo Wolde of Ethiopia wins the 1968 Marathon

Top right: The only man to retain a Marathon Olympic title – Abebe Bikila (Ethiopia) records the then fastest-ever to win in Japan in 2 hr. 12 min. 11·2 sec.
Above right: Dorando Pietri (Italy), first past the post in the 1908 Marathon, but disqualified for assistance

*No real comparison between performances is possible as courses and conditions vary so much. Prior to 1908 and in 1912 the distance was about 40,000 metres. In 1908 it was 26 miles 385 yards (42,195 metres) which distance has been accepted as "standard" since 1924. In 1920 it was 42,750 metres.

THE MARATHON · OLYMPIC CHAMPIONS*

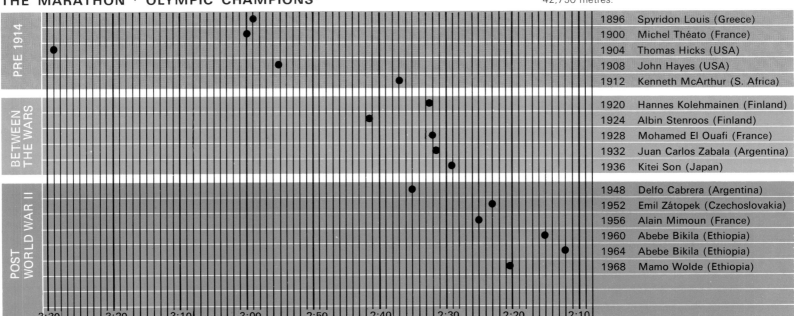

PRE 1914	1896	Spyridon Louis (Greece)
	1900	Michel Théato (France)
	1904	Thomas Hicks (USA)
	1908	John Hayes (USA)
	1912	Kenneth McArthur (S. Africa)
BETWEEN THE WARS	1920	Hannes Kolehmainen (Finland)
	1924	Albin Stenroos (Finland)
	1928	Mohamed El Ouafi (France)
	1932	Juan Carlos Zabala (Argentina)
	1936	Kitei Son (Japan)
POST WORLD WAR II	1948	Delfo Cabrera (Argentina)
	1952	Emil Zátopek (Czechoslovakia)
	1956	Alain Mimoun (France)
	1960	Abebe Bikila (Ethiopia)
	1964	Abebe Bikila (Ethiopia)
	1968	Mamo Wolde (Ethiopia)

3:30   3:20   3:10   3:00   2:50   2:40   2:30   2:20   2:10

The Walks

"Walking" is defined in the *Oxford Dictionary* as "the action of moving on the feet at any pace short of breaking into a run or a trot", while the definition from the point of view of amateur athletics is: "Progression by steps so taken that unbroken contact with the ground is maintained, i.e. the advancing foot must make contact with the ground before the rear foot leaves the ground."

Long-distance walking was fashionable in the eighteenth and nineteenth centuries, though how far those engaged in it always kept unbroken contact with the ground must be a matter for considerable doubt. Particularly famous was the feat of a Captain Barclay, who in 1801 walked 300 miles in five days, and eight years later covered 1,000 miles in a thousand consecutive hours.

A 7-mile walk was included in the first British Amateur Championships in 1866, and this event continued until 1969 when it was changed to 10,000 metres. A 4-mile event was held from 1894 to 1900, when it was changed to 2 miles, and this later became a 3,000 metres event.

The Road Walking Association have held a 20-mile walk since 1908, and a 50-kilometres event since 1930, both on the road. Not until the 1908 Games in London were there any Olympic walking events. Then there were two walks at 3,500 metres and 10 miles, both won by G. E. Larner of Great Britain. At Stockholm, four years later, the only event was over 10,000 metres. After the first world war, there were again two events in 1920 — 3,000 and 10,000 metres, both won by the Italian walker, Ugo Frigerio. Ugo was extremely popular with the crowd, and a great exhibitionist who often led the applause if he was not entirely satisfied with the volume. Frigerio retained his title in the 10,000 metres at Paris in 1924, where there was no 3,000 event, but there was so much dispute among the judges that no event at all was included in the 1928 Games.

Top: Paul Nihill (GB), second, defends his 1969 European gold medal in the 20,000 metres walk in Helsinki
Left: Nikolay Smaga (USSR) wins the 20,000 metres 1971 European title from Gerhard Sperling (GDR)
Below: Noel Freeman wins the Commonwealth 20-mile walk in 2 hr. 33 min. 33 sec.

The greatly increased popularity of road walking, as contrasted with track events, led to the inclusion of a 50,000-metre event at Los Angeles, and this was won by Tommy Green of Great Britain with a lead of seven minutes over his nearest rival.

One of Britain's finest exponents, Harold Whitlock, maintained Green's success by winning the Olympic title at Berlin in 1936. He won by over a minute, finishing in just over four and a half hours.

After the second world war, the 10,000 metres was reintroduced for two Olympics, and the 50,000 metres repeated. On each occasion, Sweden provided the winners in both events, the gold medallist in the short track event being J. Mikaelsson. He retained his title four years later, in the last track walk to feature in the Games.

In the 50,000 metres, the Italian, Dordini, beat four and a half hours for the first time.

Then, in Melbourne 1956, Russia secured all three Olympic medals in the newly introduced 20,000 metres, with Englishman Norman Read winning the 50,000 metres race for New Zealand. Golubnichiy won the 20,000 metres with just under ten seconds to spare, and two Olympics later in Mexico, he repeated this success. Meantime, in Tokyo, Ken Matthews from Great Britain won the 20,000 metres gold, with the Russian, Golubnichiy third.

In Rome 1960, Great Britain's diminutive Don Thompson, who four years before had dropped out of the 50,000-metre race, won that event by a mere seventeen seconds, from the Swede Ljunggren who had won the event in London twelve years previously.

In Mexico 1968, the East German, Christoph Hohne, led the 50,000-metre event from start to finish to win by over ten minutes in 4 hr. 20 min. 13·6 sec. Considering the great disadvantage of walking over thirty-one miles at a height of more than 7,000 feet, this performance was most remarkable.

The unofficial world record for one mile is 6 min. 15·2 sec., and Britain's greatest long-distance walker ever, Paul Nihill, has walked the distance in only one and eight-tenths of a second slower, equating to an average speed of 9·6 miles per hour. Nihill finished nineteen seconds behind Pamich in the 1964 Olympic 50,000 metres, and he also won the 20,000 metres at the 1969 European Championships.

Another Russian victory over East Germany. Venyamin Soldatenko beat world record-holder and Olympic champion Christoph Hohne, to win the 50,000 metres (31¼ miles) European walk in two and a half minutes outside four hours

THE WALKS · OLYMPIC CHAMPIONS

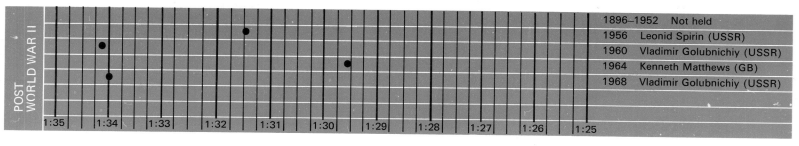

1896–1952	Not held
1956	Leonid Spirin (USSR)
1960	Vladimir Golubnichiy (USSR)
1964	Kenneth Matthews (GB)
1968	Vladimir Golubnichiy (USSR)

1:35 1:34 1:33 1:32 1:31 1:30 1:29 1:28 1:27 1:26 1:25

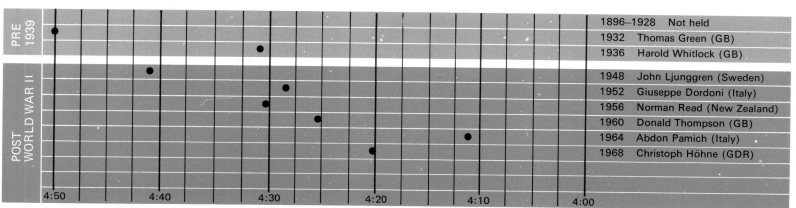

1896–1928	Not held
1932	Thomas Green (GB)
1936	Harold Whitlock (GB)
1948	John Ljunggren (Sweden)
1952	Giuseppe Dordoni (Italy)
1956	Norman Read (New Zealand)
1960	Donald Thompson (GB)
1964	Abdon Pamich (Italy)
1968	Christoph Höhne (GDR)

4:50 4:40 4:30 4:20 4:10 4:00

The Steeplechase

Originally, a "steeplechase" was a race on horses across country, but the steeplechases across country on foot became the feature of many schools' sports. Such an event was included in the very first Oxford and Cambridge sports, in 1864. Then, a steeplechase of sorts was included in the first British Amateur Championships in 1880, and the distance was eventually standardised in Britain in 1913, at two miles. Just before the second world war other conditions, such as the number of hurdles and the size of the water jump, were introduced.

Even though a steeplechase event featured in the Olympic Games as early as 1900, it was not until 1954 that the International Federation laid down specific rules and accepted the event as eligible for a world record. Today, the standard event is over 3,000 metres, which is two hundred and forty yards short of two miles, and must include twenty-eight clearances of 3 ft. high hurdles, four per lap, and seven water jumps taken one per lap.

In 1920, the first Olympic race over 3,000 metres was held, resulting in a win for Percy Hodge, the British champion.

At Amsterdam, in the 1928 Games, the event really became more of an obstacle race when the construction of the water jump made it possible for an athlete to put his foot on the top of the hurdle and clear the water. Previously, he had to leap over the hedge, and almost always landed in the water, though Lord Burghley once delighted a crowd by leaping right over both the hedge and the water. It was Paavo Nurmi who originated the technique of stepping on the hurdle, and he finished second to Loukola of Finland in the 1928 Olympic steeplechase.

There was an unusual incident in the 1932 Olympic race, when an error was made by the official responsible for counting the laps, and an extra lap was run. The winner, Iso-Hollo of Finland, had already set up a new Olympic record of 9 min. 14·6 sec. in his heat, and he retained his title in 1936 with an Olympic record, this time of 9 min. 03·8 sec.

The 1952 Olympics produced the first victory inside nine minutes, when the American Horace Ashenfelter beat Vladimir Kazantsev of U.S.S.R. by six seconds, in 8 min. 45·4 sec. John Disley of Great Britain was third, but only one-fifth of a second behind the Russian, and all the first seven runners beat nine minutes.

In 1954, the I.A.A.F. standardised conditions, and in the next two years before the Melbourne Olympics, the improvement in steeplechasing was exceptional. In September 1956. Sandor Rozsnoyi reduced the world record to 8 min. 35·6 sec. He reached the Olympic final in Melbourne, when the race resulted in a surprise victory for Christopher Brasher of Great Britain, an athlete who had never won a major race before. His gold medal was not secured without a struggle, for at first he was disqualified following an allegation that he had interfered with another competitor. However, the Jury of Appeal reinstated him as the winner after a long inquiry.

In Mexico 1968, the Olympic event was certainly very much affected by the altitude. Gaston Roelants, who had previously set up a world record of 8 min. 26·4 sec., only just beat nine minutes to finish in seventh position at the Games. The first two, Biwott and Kogo came from Kenya, the former delighting the huge crowd by his performance of completely clearing the water jump on each occasion. The story was that he did not wish to get his new shoes wet.

In 1969, Dudin of Russia brought the world record down to 8 min. 22·2 sec., while in 1970 Kerry O'Brien of Australia did 8 min. 22·0 sec.

Amos Biwott delighted the crowds by clearing the water jump when winning the Mexican steeplechase by less than one second from fellow-Kenyan Benjamin Koge

Above: Twenty-five years after — Jean-Paul Villain brings the European steeplechase title back to France with a new championship record of 8 min. 25·2 sec. France's previous winner, Raphael Pujazon in 1946, was thirty-six seconds slower

Top left: Gaston Roelants (Bel) leads in the Tokyo steeplechase which he won from Maurice Herriott (GB) in the new Olympic record time of 8 min. 30·8 sec. The record still stands

Above: Only a lap to go, but world record-holder Kerry O'Brien (No. 25) falls at the water jump and fellow-Australian Tony Manning (No. 22) wins the "gold" in 8 min. 26·2 sec. — a new Commonwealth Games record, but 4·2 sec. slower than the world best

THE STEEPLECHASE · OLYMPIC CHAMPIONS

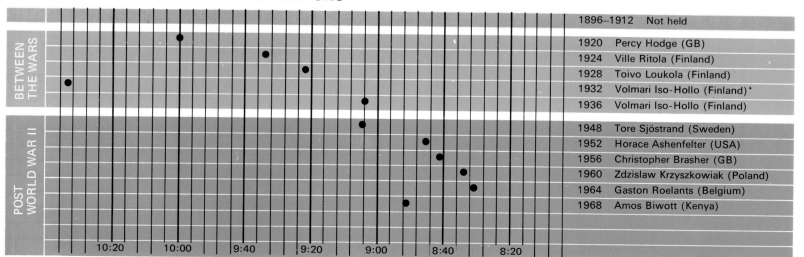

BETWEEN THE WARS	1896–1912	Not held
	1920	Percy Hodge (GB)
	1924	Ville Ritola (Finland)
	1928	Toivo Loukola (Finland)
	1932	Volmari Iso-Hollo (Finland)*
	1936	Volmari Iso-Hollo (Finland)
POST WORLD WAR II	1948	Tore Sjöstrand (Sweden)
	1952	Horace Ashenfelter (USA)
	1956	Christopher Brasher (GB)
	1960	Zdzislaw Krzyszkowiak (Poland)
	1964	Gaston Roelants (Belgium)
	1968	Amos Biwott (Kenya)

Time axis: 10:20 10:00 9:40 9:20 9:00 8:40 8:20

* By mistake an extra lap was run.

110 Metres Hurdles

While the height of hurdles for the imperial event over 120 yards was historically determined because it was the height of sheep hurdles generally in use in Great Britain, there is no obvious explanation as to why they were placed ten yards apart, or why the distance was 120 yards, with fifteen yards to the start, and the same distance from the last hurdle to the finish. The original hurdles were driven into the ground, so that it was practically impossible to knock one over. Later, hurdles were constructed which stood on the ground, and by 1920 a rule had been introduced which led to the disqualification of a competitor who knocked down three hurdles, and the disallowance of a record if even one hurdle was toppled over.

By 1936, however, the weight of hurdles had been officially laid down, and nowadays a hurdler is neither disqualified nor is the record disallowed, no matter how many hurdles are knocked over. But it is, of course, a disadvantage for a top-class hurdler to hit a hurdle, because it breaks his rhythm and must reduce his speed.

A hurdle event was included in the 1896 Games, but then the distance was over 100 metres. The hurdles were one metre high — 3 ft. 3 in. — and there were only eight, so that this can hardly be in any way comparable to the standard event as eventually introduced in 1900, over 110 metres.

At first, the hurdler was inclined to jump the hurdles, but gradually a highly skilled technique has been evolved and improved upon.

In 1971, an American, Rod Milburn, covered 120 yards in the almost unbelievable time of 13·0 sec. exactly. This means that, allowing an extra tenth of a second for each hurdle, he ran the distance in even time !

The success of the Americans in the Olympic Games in this event has been pronounced. In the fifteen contests, that is ignoring 1896, they claim thirteen victories and a total of thirty-seven places in the first three, out of a possible forty-five.

The only other countries to provide a winner in the Olympic 110 metres, are Canada and South Africa. In 1920, Canadian-born — but American-trained — Earl Thomson became the first man to beat fifteen seconds, winning in 14·8 sec. This was also a new world record.

Throughout the years, only one British athlete has gained an Olympic medal in this event. He was Group Captain Donald Finlay, third in 1932, and then second, four years later. His bronze medal was awarded only after a photographic record had been examined,

Eight in a row — Willie Davenport maintains the Americans' unbroken series of victories in the 110 metres hurdles since 1932. Davenport was also the fifth successive Negro to win this event

for at first the third place had been awarded to an American. Finlay, who was Britain's top hurdler for almost twenty years, won the British hurdles title on eight occasions, and on his final appearance at the age of forty, he covered the distance in 14·4 sec.

Up to the first world war, the Americans had always secured the first three places in this event, a success which they repeated in the first four Games after the second world war.

Alvin Kraenzlein, who won four gold medals at the 1900 Games, was the first hurdler to use the modern high-hurdling technique. His time of 15·2 sec. remained a world best for nine years. He also held world records for the 220 yards low hurdles and the long jump.

Of world record-holders from 1908 to 1971, the U.S.A. claim thirteen, Sweden two, Canada, Finland, Germany and South Africa one each.

Lee Calhoun (USA), the only man to win the 110 metres hurdles on two occasions (1956 and 1960)

Olympic 400 metres hurdles champion, David Hemery, wins the Commonwealth 110 metres hurdles title

110 METRES HURDLES · OLYMPIC CHAMPIONS

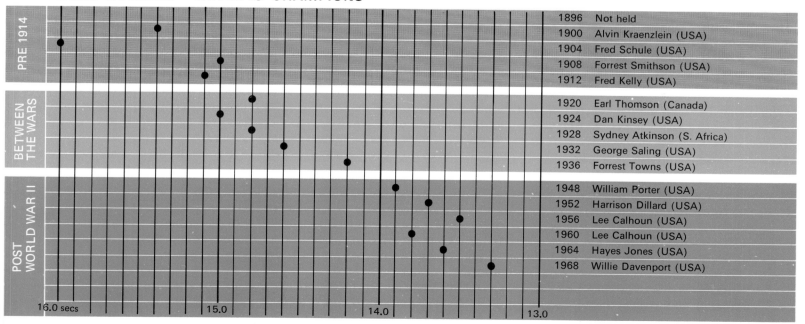

	Year	Champion
PRE 1914	1896	Not held
	1900	Alvin Kraenzlein (USA)
	1904	Fred Schule (USA)
	1908	Forrest Smithson (USA)
	1912	Fred Kelly (USA)
BETWEEN THE WARS	1920	Earl Thomson (Canada)
	1924	Dan Kinsey (USA)
	1928	Sydney Atkinson (S. Africa)
	1932	George Saling (USA)
	1936	Forrest Towns (USA)
POST WORLD WAR II	1948	William Porter (USA)
	1952	Harrison Dillard (USA)
	1956	Lee Calhoun (USA)
	1960	Lee Calhoun (USA)
	1964	Hayes Jones (USA)
	1968	Willie Davenport (USA)

16.0 secs   15.0   14.0   13.0

400 Metres Hurdles

A 400 metres hurdles event, over ten flights each 3 ft. high, and thirty-five metres, or thirty-eight yards, apart, was included in the 1900 Games in Paris, repeated with 2 ft. 6 in. hurdles in St. Louis, and then in London in 1908. It was not included in the British Championships until 1914, and first became featured in the U.S.A. in the same year. By contrast, in the U.S.A. inter-collegiate matches, a 220 yards hurdles event with the obstacles 2 ft. 6 in. high, was held as long ago as 1888, and such an event over metres was included in the 1900 and 1904 Olympics.

In the twelve races in the Olympic Games since 1908, the United States has won nine gold medals, Great Britain two and the Irish Free State one.

The British victories were achieved at a forty-year interval. In 1928, Lord Burghley, later to become the Marquis of Exeter and President of the International Amateur Athletic Federation, won despite competition from the 1924 Olympic champion and world record-holder, F. Morgan Taylor. In 1968, David Hemery gained one of the most exciting and brilliant victories in the whole history of the Games, when he won by nine-tenths of a second in 48·1 sec. — a world record.

A world record was set up in the London Olympics in 1908, when the American Charles Bacon clocked 55·0 sec. to finish about a yard ahead of his fellow-countryman Harry Hillman, winner of this event and two others in 1904.

In Paris, 1924, Morgan Taylor won the Olympic event in 52·6 sec., but he knocked down the last hurdle and, as the rules then stood, the record could not be accepted. In Los Angeles, the same fate fell to Robert Tisdall of Eire. He won a superb race a couple of yards ahead of Glenn Hardin (U.S.A.) in 51·7 sec. when the existing world record was 52·0 sec.

The Olympic record was improved upon in 1948, 1952, 1956 and 1960. Outstanding was the repeat victory of American Glenn Davis in Melbourne in 1956, and Rome in 1960. American athletes finished in the first three places on both occasions.

In 1956, the South African Gerhardus Potgieter, nineteen years of age and quite inexperienced in top-class international competition, was almost certain to gain the bronze medal until he fell at the last hurdle. The following year, he set up a new world record for the imperial 440 yards hurdles of 50·7 sec. Then, in 1958, when winning the Commonwealth title, he managed 49·7 sec. In April 1960 Potgieter reduced his world record to 49·3 sec. on his twenty-third birthday, and certainly seemed in the running for the Olympic gold in Rome. Tragically he was involved in a car accident in Germany a short time before the Olympics, sustaining major injuries which prevented his competing in the Rome Games.

Apart from Britain's two gold medals — Burghley and Hemery — John Cooper gained a silver medal in the 1964 Olympics, and John Sherwood a bronze in 1968. John Sherwood lost second place by literally a neck, for it was Gerhard Hennige of Germany's "neck" which gave him the verdict. A few days later, the I.A.A.F. altered the rules and the "neck" is not now counted as part of the "torso", and it is the torso which decides when an athlete has reached the finish line. Under the present rule, Sherwood would be a silver medallist.

It seems probable that in the not too distant future the world record will be inside 48·0 sec. It took over twenty years for the world record to be reduced from inside 51·0 sec. to inside 50·0 sec., and then twelve years more to get inside 49·0 sec.

Above: John Sherwood (Eng), Commonwealth 400 metres hurdles winner. He was third in the Olympic event two years previously

Below: A French victory at the Helsinki European Championships, where Jean-Claude Nallet leads two Russians to win in 49·2 sec.

Above: Within seconds of the finish, David Hemery's world record for the 400 metres hurdles appears on the board

Right: Probably the greatest track achievement of the 1968 Olympics. David Hemery (GB) won the 400 metres hurdles by nearly ten yards and beat the previous world record by seven-tenths of a second

Below: South Africa's Gert Potgieter winning the 1958 440 yards Commonwealth title in the then world record time of 49·7 sec. This was the last occasion on which South African athletes appeared in the Commonwealth Games

400 METRES HURDLES · OLYMPIC CHAMPIONS

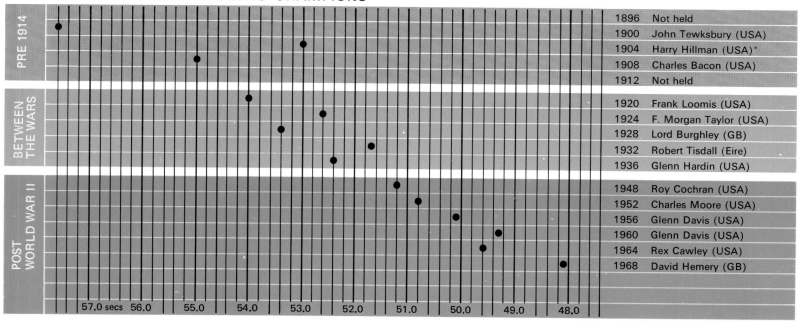

PRE 1914	1896	Not held
	1900	John Tewksbury (USA)
	1904	Harry Hillman (USA)*
	1908	Charles Bacon (USA)
	1912	Not held
BETWEEN THE WARS	1920	Frank Loomis (USA)
	1924	F. Morgan Taylor (USA)
	1928	Lord Burghley (GB)
	1932	Robert Tisdall (Eire)
	1936	Glenn Hardin (USA)
POST WORLD WAR II	1948	Roy Cochran (USA)
	1952	Charles Moore (USA)
	1956	Glenn Davis (USA)
	1960	Glenn Davis (USA)
	1964	Rex Cawley (USA)
	1968	David Hemery (GB)

57.0 secs 56.0 55.0 54.0 53.0 52.0 51.0 50.0 49.0 48.0

* In 1904 the race was run over 2 ft. 6 in. not 3 ft. hurdles.

4 x 100 Metres Relay

In the twelve contests held, the United States have won ten Olympic gold medals. They were disqualified in 1912, and again in 1960, on the latter occasion after finishing first in the final. They were also disqualified in 1948 in London, when the race was awarded to Great Britain. But, after the Jury of Appeal had examined a film of the race, it became clear that the disqualification was an error, and the decision of the referee was reversed.

Throughout the fifty-six years since 1912, when the event was introduced into the Games, the world record has almost invariably been beaten in the Olympics.

In 1924, Great Britain's team set up a new world record of 42·0 sec. in the heats, but in the final the United States did 41·0 sec. and Great Britain 41·2 sec. Eight years later, the United States achieved 40·0 sec. — an "even-time" performance — and in the last Olympics before the second world war, in Berlin in 1936, they produced a time of 39·8 sec.

The American success in Tokyo, 1964, was due to a fantastic last leg by Bob Hayes who was that year's Olympic 100 metres winner as well as being the first man to run 100 yards in 9·1 sec. The Americans set a new world record of 39·0 sec., but four years later, in the favourable climatic conditions of Mexico City, the Jamaicans reduced the record to 38·3 sec. This performance was in the semi-final, but in the final they finished fourth in 38·4 sec. Again, it was largely due to the "anchor" stage by the Olympic champion Jim Hines, that the United States won in the new world record time of 38·2 sec., which is an average speed of about 23½ m.p.h.

The modern rules of relay racing provide that the baton must be between eleven and twelve inches long, weighing one and three-quarter ounces and have a circumference of four and three-quarter inches. It must be exchanged within a zone of twenty metres, or twenty-two yards. In races up to 4×220 yards, the runner receiving the baton may commence running not more than eleven yards outside the take-over zone.

Judging whether the baton has been passed within the zone can be a difficult matter. At Munich a video tape of the race will be available if required.

Facing page, top left: Last change in the 4×100 metres at Helsinki. First, Czechoslovakia (39·3 sec.); second, Poland (39·7 sec.); fourth, Great Britain (39·8 sec.). And (top right) the ecstasy of victory for two of the winners

Facing page, bottom: Jamaica's winning sprint relay team in Edinburgh. Their time – 39·8 sec.

Above: Jim Hines takes the United States to a world record victory in the Mexico Olympics in 38·2 sec. Cuba were second (38·3 sec.) and France third (38·4 sec.). The first six teams beat the previous Olympic record of 39·0 sec.

4×100 METRES RELAY · OLYMPIC CHAMPIONS

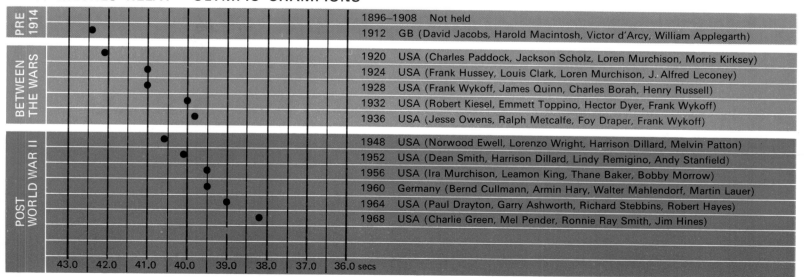

		1896–1908	Not held
PRE 1914		1912	GB (David Jacobs, Harold Macintosh, Victor d'Arcy, William Applegarth)
BETWEEN THE WARS		1920	USA (Charles Paddock, Jackson Scholz, Loren Murchison, Morris Kirksey)
		1924	USA (Frank Hussey, Louis Clark, Loren Murchison, J. Alfred Leconey)
		1928	USA (Frank Wykoff, James Quinn, Charles Borah, Henry Russell)
		1932	USA (Robert Kiesel, Emmett Toppino, Hector Dyer, Frank Wykoff)
		1936	USA (Jesse Owens, Ralph Metcalfe, Foy Draper, Frank Wykoff)
POST WORLD WAR II		1948	USA (Norwood Ewell, Lorenzo Wright, Harrison Dillard, Melvin Patton)
		1952	USA (Dean Smith, Harrison Dillard, Lindy Remigino, Andy Stanfield)
		1956	USA (Ira Murchison, Leamon King, Thane Baker, Bobby Morrow)
		1960	Germany (Bernd Cullmann, Armin Hary, Walter Mahlendorf, Martin Lauer)
		1964	USA (Paul Drayton, Garry Ashworth, Richard Stebbins, Robert Hayes)
		1968	USA (Charlie Green, Mel Pender, Ronnie Ray Smith, Jim Hines)
43.0	42.0	41.0	40.0	39.0	38.0	37.0	36.0 secs

4x400 Metres Relay

A relay race was first introduced into the Olympics programme in 1908, when the distance was 1,600 metres — two stages of 200 metres, one of 400 and one of 800 metres. It was in 1912 that the event was changed to 4×400 metres.

Of the twelve competitions held over 4×400 metres, nine have been won by the U.S.A., two by Britain and one by Jamaica. On eight occasions the winning team has set up a world record. Over the sixty years since 1912, the world record has improved from 3 min. 16·6 sec. (an average of 49·15 sec. per man) to 2 min. 56·1 sec. (an average of 44·025 sec.), an improvement of over five seconds per man. During the same period, the individual world record has improved from 47·8 sec. to 43·8 sec.

The world record for the relay has been broken eleven times in the sixty years. Only once has a non-U.S.A. team gained the distinction — the Jamaican team in 1952, which, with Arthur Wint, Les Laing, Herbert McKenley and George Rhoden, beat the U.S.A. by two yards, in 3 min. 03·9 sec. This record stood for eight years.

Great Britain won from South Africa in 1920, and four years later in Paris, an American team defeated Sweden by one second in a new world record time of 3 min. 16 sec. Great Britain who finished third, were without Eric Liddell, who was not prepared to compete on a Sunday.

Two more victories for the U.S.A. resulted in 1928 and 1932, again with new world records. In 1932, the Americans averaged just outside 47 sec., six seconds faster than their previous world record made in 1928. Great Britain were also inside the previous world record, with Lord Burghley covering his stage in 46·7 sec.

Great Britain had an exhilarating victory in Berlin in 1936, finishing fifteen yards ahead of the U.S.A. and only four-fifths of a second outside the existing world record.

The U.S.A. gained a very easy victory in 1948, when over the third leg, Arthur Wint chasing Roy Cochran pulled up lame. The same Jamaican team — Wint, Laing, McKenley, Rhoden — gained a fine revenge in 1952 in the world record time of 3 min. 03·9 sec., an average of just outside 46 sec.

The Americans won the event in the next three Games — 1960 in Rome, 1964 in Tokyo and 1968 in Mexico. In Rome, there was a great battle between the U.S.A. and Germany. A lap by Glenn Davis of 45·4 sec., gave American namesake and 400-metre champion Otis Davis about a six-yard lead over Carl Kaufmann, with whom Davis shared a new world 400 metres record in the individual final two days before. Kaufmann slightly reduced the lead.

Four years later in Tokyo, the U.S.A. beat Great Britain by nine-tenths of a second, and seven-tenths of a second outside three minutes. A great run by Robbie Brightwell, Captain of the British Men's Athletic Team, gave his team the silver medal by a tenth of a second over Trinidad-Tobago. Both teams also beat the previous world record.

In July 1966, in a match between the U.S.A. and the Commonwealth, an American team beat three minutes for the first time, with Lee Evans returning 43·8 sec. over the final leg.

In Mexico, the U.S.A. with the three individual 400 metres medallists, Lee Evans, Larry James and Ron Freeman, won by three and a half seconds from Kenya in 2 min. 56·1 sec. Great Britain in fifth place set up a national record of 3 min. 01·2 sec.

A "gold" for Britain on the final day of the Berlin Olympics. Godfrey Rampling, after a magnificent run, hands over to Bill Roberts, and with Brown to come a British victory is assured

Helsinki 1952: the victorious Jamaican team of McKenley, Wint, Laing and Rhoden which beat the Americans by a yard in 3 min. 03·9 sec. and also beat a world record which had stood for twenty years. Arthur Wint, who ran the first leg in a vest borrowed from George Rhoden was so thrilled by McKenley's running that he only gave the vest to Rhoden seconds before he started off for the final leg.

4×400 METRES RELAY · OLYMPIC CHAMPIONS

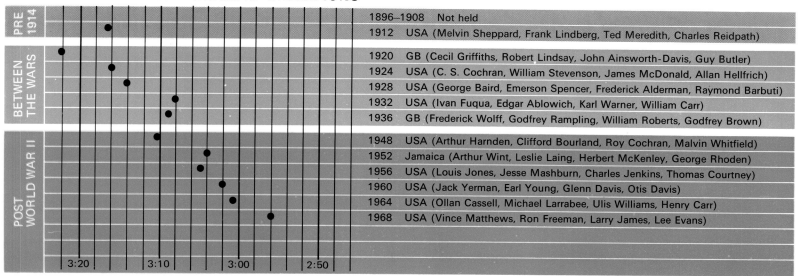

PRE 1914	1896–1908	Not held
	1912	USA (Melvin Sheppard, Frank Lindberg, Ted Meredith, Charles Reidpath)
BETWEEN THE WARS	1920	GB (Cecil Griffiths, Robert Lindsay, John Ainsworth-Davis, Guy Butler)
	1924	USA (C. S. Cochran, William Stevenson, James McDonald, Allan Helffrich)
	1928	USA (George Baird, Emerson Spencer, Frederick Alderman, Raymond Barbuti)
	1932	USA (Ivan Fuqua, Edgar Ablowich, Karl Warner, William Carr)
	1936	GB (Frederick Wolff, Godfrey Rampling, William Roberts, Godfrey Brown)
POST WORLD WAR II	1948	USA (Arthur Harnden, Clifford Bourland, Roy Cochran, Malvin Whitfield)
	1952	Jamaica (Arthur Wint, Leslie Laing, Herbert McKenley, George Rhoden)
	1956	USA (Louis Jones, Jesse Mashburn, Charles Jenkins, Thomas Courtney)
	1960	USA (Jack Yerman, Earl Young, Glenn Davis, Otis Davis)
	1964	USA (Ollan Cassell, Michael Larrabee, Ulis Williams, Henry Carr)
	1968	USA (Vince Matthews, Ron Freeman, Larry James, Lee Evans)

3:20 3:10 3:00 2:50

The Decathlon

The word "decathlon" means literally ten events. The Ancient Greeks held an all-round competition of five events, including one running event of about 200 yards, which was probably the length of the stadium. There was also a long jump, discus throw, javelin throw and wrestling, and the five-event competition was called the "pentathlon".

All-round competitions were held in Ireland from the middle of the nineteenth century, and the United States introduced a similar competition in their 1884 Championships. The Americans included ten events in their "all-round" competition. All were held on one day — the 100 yards, shot putt, high jump, 880 yards walk, hammer, pole vault, 120 yards hurdles, throwing the 56 lb. weight, long jump, and one mile. Mr. Avery Brundage, President of the International Olympic Committee since 1952, won the title three times.

The present decathlon originated in Sweden, and was included in the 1912 Olympics when the events were spread over three days. Now, they take place over two days, in the following order — *first day:* 100 metres, long jump, shot, high jump and 400 metres — *second day:* 110 metres hurdles, discus, pole vault, javelin and 1,500 metres. Each competitor scores points in each event according to a highly scientific table. The points awarded have been changed a number of times. The present table was agreed in 1962, but is due for revision.

At the 1912, 1920 and 1924 Games a pentathlon — consisting of long jump, javelin, 200 metres, discus and 1,500 metres — was also held. What is known as a "modern pentathlon" — cross-country, horse-riding, swimming, fencing and shooting — is now held, but it is not part of the track and field programme.

In 1912, an American Indian, James Thorpe, won both the decathlon and pentathlon. He was a magnificent all-round performer, winning the decathlon by 700 points and with a total score which was not surpassed for twenty years.

Some time after the Games, the United States authorities discovered that Thorpe was not an "amateur" because he had played professional baseball in 1909, and he was stripped of his gold medals.

Sweden and Norway provided the first two Olympic decathlon champions, and then in 1924, Harold Osborn, the American world high jump record-holder, not only won the high jump, but also the decathlon with over 300 points to spare.

In 1928, the Finn Paavo Yrjola, beat fellow-countryman Akilles Jarvinen, and four years later, Jarvinen had again to be content with the silver medal behind American James Bausch. It is interesting to note that under the 1962 scoring table, Jarvinen would have been the gold medallist each time.

The Americans won all three Olympic decathlon medals in 1936, Glenn Norris setting up a new world record, which was to be beaten in 1950 by Bob Mathias also of the U.S.A. Mathias is the only man successfully to defend a decathlon Olympic title. In 1948, three months before his eighteenth birthday, he gained a remarkable victory, and he retained his title in 1952 by the largest margin ever — 599 points on the new scoring and over 800 on the old.

In 1968 Bill Toomey (U.S.A.) was nearly 200 points ahead of Hans-Joachim Walde, of West Germany, with the javelin and 1,500 metres to come — and with the German world record-holder, Kurt Bendlin, in third place. Walde reduced the American's lead to 74 points in the javelin, but Toomey won by running the 1,500 metres three-fifths of a second faster than the German. In his last appearance in a decathlon event at the end of 1969, Toomey, who is now married to Olympic long jump champion Mary Rand, raised the world record to 8,417 points — 224 points more than his Olympic total and 98 more than Kurt Bendlin's previous world record.

The United Kingdom record is 7,903 points by Peter Gabbett in 1971.

Below: Bill Toomey (USA), Olympic decathlon champion in Mexico and also world record-holder with 8,417 points

Right: Geoff Smith (Aus) with a score of 7,492 points, wins the Commonwealth title by 23 points from Peter Gabbett (Eng). Smith was 252 points behind after the first five events

Above and below: Joachim Kirst (GDR) led Lennart Hedmark (Swe) by 376 points at the half-way stage, and finally with a score of 8,196 points with 158 points to spare in the ten-event 1971 European Championship

THE DECATHLON · OLYMPIC CHAMPIONS*

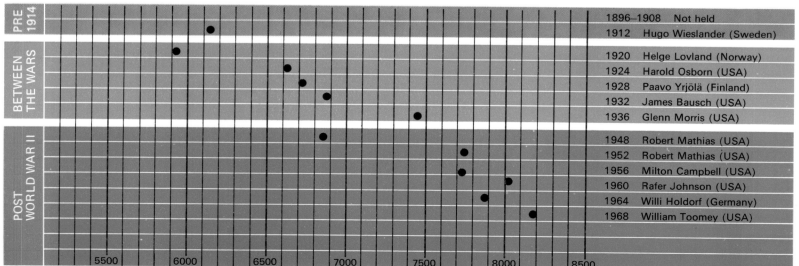

PRE 1914	1896–1908	Not held
	1912	Hugo Wieslander (Sweden)
BETWEEN THE WARS	1920	Helge Lovland (Norway)
	1924	Harold Osborn (USA)
	1928	Paavo Yrjölä (Finland)
	1932	James Bausch (USA)
	1936	Glenn Morris (USA)
POST WORLD WAR II	1948	Robert Mathias (USA)
	1952	Robert Mathias (USA)
	1956	Milton Campbell (USA)
	1960	Rafer Johnson (USA)
	1964	Willi Holdorf (Germany)
	1968	William Toomey (USA)

5500 6000 6500 7000 7500 8000 8500

* All adjusted to 1962 scoring.

Men's Field Events

Putting the shot was originally an event for soldiers, and known as putting the (cannon) ball. The athlete performed from a square and not, as now, a circle

There are nine Olympic men's field events, if we include the "decathlon" which itself consists of three track events, a hurdles and six field events. This programme was standardised in 1928.

In 1896, there were six field events — high jump, long jump, the triple jump (the winner took two hops as opposed to the present hop, step and jump), pole vault, shot and discus. Three Americans accounted for the six events, since Ellery Clark won both the high and long jumps, while Robert Garrett won the shot by three-quarters of an inch and the discus, which he had never thrown in competition before, by seven and three-quarter inches. The distance in the long jump was 20 ft. 10 in. — only two inches more than the qualifying distance for the 1972 Women's event!

The improvement in field events since the second world war has been even more remarkable than in track. I give below the Olympic records in 1936, 1952 and 1968, both in metres and in feet and inches.

	1936			1952			1968		
	metres	ft.	in.	metres	ft.	in.	metres	ft.	in.
High jump	2·03	6	8	2·04	6	8¼	2·24	7	4¼
Pole vault	4·35	14	3¼	4·55	14	11¼	5·40	17	8½
Long jump	8·06	26	5¼	8·06	26	5¼	8·90	29	2½
Triple jump	16·00	52	6	16·22	53	2½	17·39	57	0½
Shot	16·20	53	1¾	17·41	57	1½	20·54	67	4¾
Discus	50·48	165	7½	55·03	180	6½	64·78	212	6
Hammer	56·49	185	4	60·34	197	11½	73·36	240	8
Javelin	72·71	238	6½*	73·78	242	0½	90·10	295	7

* Made in 1932.

Of the eleven Olympics held since 1920, here are some of the outstanding field event performances of each Games.

The following have won their events on more than one occasion:
Pole vault: R. Richards (1952 and 1956)
Long jump: Myer Prinstein (1900 and 1904)
Triple jump: A. da Silva (1952 and 1956), J. Schmidt (1960 and 1964)
Shot: R. Rose (1904 and 1908), P. O'Brien (1952 and 1956)
Discus: M. Sheridan (1904 and 1908), C. Houser (1924 and 1928), A. Oerter (1956, 1960, 1964 and 1968)
Hammer: J. Flanagan (1900, 1904 and 1908), P. O'Callaghan (1928 and 1932)
Javelin: J. Myrra (1920 and 1924)
Decathlon: R. Mathias (1948 and 1952)

The following have been placed in the first three in three Olympics:
Pole vault: R. Richards (3rd, 1948; 1st, 1952 and 1956)
Long jump: R. Boston (1st, 1960; 2nd, 1964; 3rd, 1968)
Triple jump: V. Tuulos (1st, 1920; 3rd, 1924; 3rd, 1928)

Shot: R. Rose (1st, 1904 and 1908; 2nd; 1912). P. O'Brien (1st, 1952 and
1956; 2nd, 1960)
Discus: A. Oerter (1st, 1956, 1960, 1964 and 1968)
Hammer: J. Flanagan (1st, 1900, 1904 and 1908), M. McGrath (2nd, 1908;
1st, 1912; 2nd, 1924), G. Zsivotzky (2nd, 1960; 2nd, 1964; 1st 1968)
Javelin: G. Kulscar (3rd, 1960; 2nd, 1964; 3rd, 1968)

1920 Antwerp

The outstanding performance was the world record pole vault of 13 ft. 5 in.
by the American Frank Foss. He won by over a foot.

1924 Paris

In the long jump competition proper, two coloured Americans, William de
Hart Hubbard and Edwin Gourdin (the world record holder, and the first man
to exceed 25 ft.) occupied first and second places, the winning jump being
24 ft. 5 in. But in the pentathlon another American, Robert le Gendre, set up
a new world record of 25 ft. $5\frac{1}{2}$ in. Anthony Winter's winning leap in the
triple jump (50 ft. $11\frac{1}{4}$ in.) beat a thirteen-year-old world record by a
quarter of an inch.

1928 Amsterdam

An Olympic record in the shot when Johnny Kuck of U.S.A. became the first
man to exceed 52 ft. Clarence Houser retained his title in the discus while
in the hammer Patrick O'Callaghan gave Eire her first Olympic "gold" with a
four-inch victory over the Swede Ossian Skiold. Another country to gain a
first "gold" was Japan, when Mikio Oda won the triple jump.

1932 Los Angeles

Japan again won the triple jump, through Chuhei Nambu with a world
record of 51 ft. 7 in. In the previous October Nambu had set up a world
record for the long jump, and is the only athlete in history to have held
world records for these two events.

1936 Berlin

The long jump duel between Jesse Owens and Luz Long was the outstanding
event in the field. Both were level with 25 ft. $8\frac{3}{4}$ in., with Owens having two
more jumps and Long one. Owens cleared 26 ft. $0\frac{1}{2}$ in., Long fouled and
with his final jump, Owens did 26 ft. $5\frac{1}{4}$ in.

1948 London

In the first post-war meeting only the shot and discus produced new
Olympic records.

1952 Helsinki

Every field event, except the long jump, produced new Olympic records, and
the triple jump a world record. Parry O'Brien, who was destined to raise the
world record for the shot by eight stages to over 63 ft., won that event by
only three-quarters of an inch with a putt of 57 ft. $1\frac{1}{2}$ in. — nearly a foot
further than the previous record.

1956 Melbourne

Olympic records in every field event except the long jump. Repeat wins by
O'Brien in the shot, Bob Richards in the pole vault and da Silva in the triple
jump. Charles Dumas, who in the previous June had become the first man to
clear 7 ft., won that event with 6 ft. $11\frac{1}{2}$ in., while in the hammer the first
six beat the previous Olympic record, and Hal Connolly won by six inches
with 207 ft. $3\frac{1}{2}$ in.

1960 Rome

Olympic records in all eight field events. Ralph Boston won the long jump by
three-quarters of an inch with 26 ft. $7\frac{3}{4}$ in., beating Jesse Owens's 1936
Olympic record by two and a half inches.

1964 Tokyo

Again Olympic records in most of the field events — over 7 ft. in the high
jump, 200 ft. in the discus (with Al Oerter winning for the third time). The
fibreglass pole produced nearly 17 ft. in the pole vault.

1968 Mexico

The most sensational memory of these Games will be the 29 ft. $2\frac{1}{2}$ in. in the
long jump. The fact that Ralph Boston broke a new Olympic record in the
qualifying round (27 ft. $1\frac{3}{4}$ in.) was completely forgotten by Beamon's
fantastic feat. Al Oerter gained his fourth successive "gold" — an
unprecedented achievement.

*Jesse Owens winning the 1936 Olympic long jump
title with a leap of 26 ft. $5\frac{1}{4}$ in. — three inches less
than his world record jump of 1935, which stood
for a quarter of a century*

High Jump

When, in March 1876, an athlete called Marshall Brooks cleared the first authentic six feet in the high jump, and three weeks later added two and a half inches to his previous "world record", there was a good deal of scepticism about the validity of the performances. In those days, "neither diving nor somersaulting" was permitted. The jump was a straightforward spring, and a "fair jump" was one "where the head of the contestant does not go over the bar before the feet, and is not below the buttocks in clearing the bar".

The only restriction nowadays is that the competitor must not take off from both feet, so that perhaps very few of the modern styles of high jumping would have been allowed in the "good old days".

At the time of the first Olympic Games in 1896, the world record was the 6 ft. 5½ in. jumped by an Irish-American, Mike Sweeney. A similar height was said to have been cleared by George Rowdon in 1890, but the record was never accepted by the A.A.A. His greatest height in winning three British championships was only six feet.

In March 1912, American George Horine appeared with a new style. It is said that his so-called "Western Roll" was developed because a pit in his garden forced him to take off with the foot nearer to the bar. But Horine's world record of 6 ft. 7 in. stood for two years.

In 1941, employing a "straddle" jump, which is crossing the bar with the front of the body facing it, Lester Steers of the U.S.A. was

within an inch of seven feet. But it was another fifteen years before a coloured American, Charles Dumas, became the first genuine seven-footer.

A year later, Russian Yuriy Stepanov broke the American monopoly of the world high jump record. He wore a "built-up" shoe, which was subsequently banned by the I.A.A.F., but his record of 7 ft. 1 in. was left in the books.

In the fifteen years since the first seven-foot leap, this height has become commonplace, though no United Kingdom performer has yet cleared it.

Since 1896, the United States have produced twelve Olympic winners and a total of twenty-eight out of forty-eight medals. In London in 1948, for the first time, the U.S.A.

Below left: With a "straddle" Lawrie Peckham (Aus) cleared 7 ft. 0¼ in. to win the 1970 Commonwealth title, the first time seven feet was cleared in the Games

Above: By clearing 7 ft. 2½ in. with his first try, Kestutis Shapka (USSR) captured the 1971 European title. For the first time a "Fosbury flop" had won the European title

Below right: After eight years Pete Matzdorf (USA) raises the world record by half an inch to 7 ft. 6¼ in. It is fifteen years since seven feet was first cleared

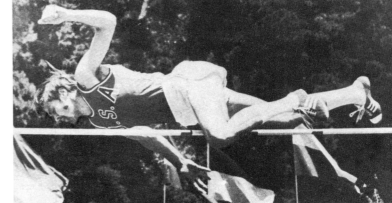

had to be content with third place, behind John Winter, of Australia, and a Norwegian; but in 1952, the Americans were again first and second.

The Melbourne Games in 1956 produced a thrilling contest, lasting five hours, with a twenty-year-old Australian, Charles Porter challenging Charles Dumas, the world record-holder. Dumas eventually cleared 6 ft. 11½ in. at his third attempt. Porter was just behind him, having jumped two and a half inches higher than ever before. A Russian in third place gave a hint of the shape of things to come from U.S.S.R. competitors in this event.

Below and right: An Olympic record for Dick Fosbury (USA), who cleared all heights up to 7 ft. 3½ in. without a fault and got over 7 ft 4¼ in. at his third attempt. The so-called "Fosbury flop" would have been banned under the original high jump rules. In the opinion of some it is more of a gymnastic trick than true high-jumping.

HIGH JUMP · OLYMPIC CHAMPIONS

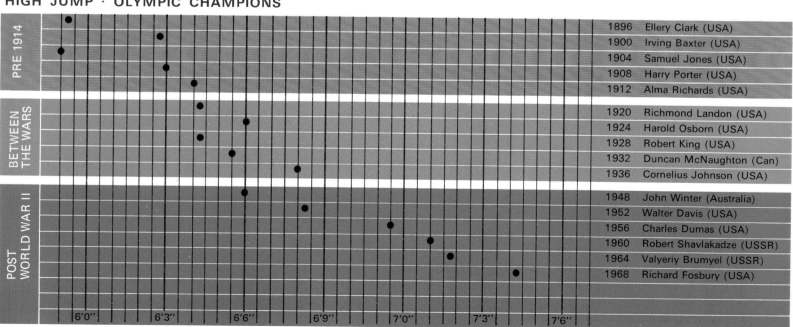

PRE 1914		1896	Ellery Clark (USA)	
		1900	Irving Baxter (USA)	
		1904	Samuel Jones (USA)	
		1908	Harry Porter (USA)	
		1912	Alma Richards (USA)	
BETWEEN THE WARS		1920	Richmond Landon (USA)	
		1924	Harold Osborn (USA)	
		1928	Robert King (USA)	
		1932	Duncan McNaughton (Can)	
		1936	Cornelius Johnson (USA)	
POST WORLD WAR II		1948	John Winter (Australia)	
		1952	Walter Davis (USA)	
		1956	Charles Dumas (USA)	
		1960	Robert Shavlakadze (USSR)	
		1964	Valyeriy Brumyel (USSR)	
		1968	Richard Fosbury (USA)	

6'0"   6'3"   6'6"   6'9"   7'0"   7'3"   7'6"

Pole Vault

Pole vaulting over a distance was practised in Germany early in the nineteenth century, but vaulting for height was started about 120 years ago in England's Lake District. The poles used were made of ash or hickory, with a spike at the end which was planted into the ground.

The pole vault was included in the first A.A.A. Championships and by the time of the first Olympics, the British record had reached 11 ft. 9 in., with the American record some six inches less. There were two Americans and three Greek competitors at Athens in 1896. The winner, W. Hoyt, cleared 10 ft. 10 in., two inches higher than his fellow American, and the three Greeks cleared just over nine feet.

From the first Games until the Mexico Olympics, the Americans have never failed to provide the gold medallist. Of the forty-eight medals won, the U.S.A. claimed thirty-three, and on four occasions Americans have filled the first three places. In 1908, two Americans shared the title with 12 ft. 2 in. each — but nowadays a tie is never allowed in the Games, and an elaborate system used to determine the outright winner.

During the second world war, Cornelius Warmerdam became the first man to vault 15 ft. Between April 1940 and June 1944, Warmerdam cleared 15 ft. forty times, and his world record of 15 ft. 7¾ in., made with a bamboo pole, remained unbeaten for fifteen years. It was finally eclipsed by Bob Gutowski, using a steel pole, in April 1957.

Robert Richards, known as "the vaulting vicar", was third in the 1948 Games with a modest 13 ft. 9½ in. But he won the gold medal in 1952 by two inches with a new Olympic record of 14 ft. 11¼ in., and four years later retained the title with 14 ft. 11½ in.

The 1960 competition was another long-drawn-out affair. After seven hours, Don Bragg, who earlier in the year had set up a new world record of 15 ft. 9¼ in., won with 15 ft. 5 in.

The 1960s saw the advent of the fibreglass pole. There can be little doubt that had the I.A.A.F. appreciated that this new pole would entirely change the event, they would have banned its use. But the manufacture and use of this artificially constructed implement had gained such widespread popularity by the time the matter was up for discussion, that the I.A.A.F. had no option but to recognise its employment.

By the time of the Tokyo Olympics, in October 1964, the world record had been raised to over 17 ft. and more than sixty people had beaten the 1960 Olympic record of 15 ft. 5 in. Of the thirty-six world records made since 1912, four went to the Norwegian, Charles Hoff, from 1922 to 1925; one to the Finn, Pentti Nikula, in 1962, and one each to Wolfgang Nordwig (GDR) and the Greek Christos Papanikolaou, the first man to clear 18 ft.

It took thirteen years to get from 14 ft. to 15 ft., and twenty-two years from 15 ft. to 16 ft. But after the introduction of the fibreglass pole, it took only fourteen months to get from 16 ft. to 16 ft. 6 in., another eleven weeks to get from 16 ft. 6 in. to 17 ft.; three years from 17 ft. to 17 ft. 6 in. and another four years from 17 ft. 6 in. to 18 ft.

Only once has a competitor from Great Britain appeared in the first six in the Olympics. He was Richard Webster, the first Britisher to clear 13 ft., which he did when sharing sixth place in the 1936 Olympics. Geoff Elliott was the first British athlete to clear 14 ft., and Trevor Burton 15 ft. United Kingdom record holder Mike Bull cleared 15 ft. 6 in. in 1966, 15 ft. 9 in. in 1967, 16 ft. 7½ in. in 1968, and 16 ft. 8¾ in. in 1970.

Three men vaulted 17 ft. 8½ in. at the Mexico Olympics, but under the rules America's Bob Seagren gained the "gold" because he made the clearance at only his second attempt, while his rivals needed three jumps each. A month earlier Seagren had set up a world record of 17 ft. 9 in. With his Mexico victory he maintained America's unbeaten Olympic record in the pole vault since 1896

Below: Don Bragg (USA), who won the Olympic title in 1960 with 15 ft. 5 in. Two months earlier he had set up a new world record of 15 ft. 9¼ in. with a steel pole – the last record before the fibreglass era. Right: Wolfgang Nordwig (GDR), three times European champion in 1966, 1969 and 1971, and briefly world record-holder in 1970 with 17 ft. 11 in.

Fred Hansen (USA) cleared 16 ft. 8¾ in. with his third jump to win the 1964 Olympic title with just two inches to spare – the first fibreglass Olympic victory. Three months earlier he had raised the world record to 17 ft. 4 in.

Mike Bull (NI), 1970 Commonwealth champion with a new United Kingdom national record of 16 ft. 8¾ in.

Christos Papanikolaou of Greece, the first man to clear eighteen feet in the pole vault, and the first Greek athlete to achieve a world record. He also holds the United Kingdom All-comers' record with 17 ft. 4½ in. He was fourth in the Mexico Olympics

POLE VAULT · OLYMPIC CHAMPIONS

1896	William Hoyt (USA)	
1900	Irving Baxter (USA)	
1904	Charles Dvorak (USA)	
1908	Alfred Gilbert and Edward Cooke (USA)	
1912	Harry Babcock (USA)	
1920	Frank Foss (USA)	
1924	Lee Barnes (USA)	
1928	Sabin Carr (USA)	
1932	William Miller (USA)	
1936	Earle Meadows (USA)	
1948	Guinn Smith (USA)	
1952	Robert Richards (USA)	
1956	Robert Richards (USA)	
1960	Donald Bragg (USA)	
1964	Fred Hansen (USA)	
1968	Robert Seagren (USA)	

PRE 1914

BETWEEN THE WARS

POST WORLD WAR II

11'0" 12'0" 13'0" 14'0" 15'0" 16'0" 17'0" 18'0"

Long Jump

Long jumping was practised by the Ancient Greeks, but mainly with the use of weights, which must have helped them to leap enormous distances. It is recorded, for example, that an Englishman using 5 lb. dumb-bells, which were thrown away while he was in mid-air, jumped 29 ft. 7 in. in May 1854.

The long jump, or "wide" jump as it was then named, was one of the events in the first Oxford and Cambridge sports, and it was also in the first United States Championships, although called the "broad" jump. The winning distances in those early days would have enabled the modern woman jumper to gain the male championship.

Twenty-three feet was first reached in 1874, and in July 1891 the American, C. S. Reber, jumped 23 ft. 6½ in. In 1893, Charles Burgess Fry, one of the finest all-round athletes Britain has ever produced, equalled Reber's world record.

Towards the end of the nineteenth century, Irishmen William Newburn and Peter O'Connor, and the Americans Alvin Kraenzlein and Myer Prinstein cleared 24 ft. The Americans finished first and second in the 1900 Olympics, Kraenzlein winning the gold with a leap of 23 ft. 6¾ in. In the previous year, both Kraenzlein and Newburn had beaten 24 ft. – and only three months before the Paris Olympics, Prinstein had captured the world record with 24 ft. 7¼ in. Peter O'Connor added another half-inch to the record at the end of August 1900, and twelve months later got to within a quarter of an inch of 25 ft., a world record which remained for just short of twenty-one years.

In July 1928, the American Edward Hamm cleared 25 ft. 11 in. and at the end of the month won the Olympic gold with a new Games record of 25 ft. 4½ in. Some six inches behind was Sylvio Cator, who in September became the first 26-footer and the only athlete from Haiti ever to hold a world record.

Jesse Owens set up a new world record of 26 ft. 8¼ in. in 1935 — and this was to remain on the books for a quarter of a century. He then won the Olympic title the following year in one of the most exciting contests ever held in the Games. In the second round of the contest Owens cleared 25 ft. 9¾ in., which the German Luz Long equalled with his fifth effort. But Owens then reached 26 ft. 0¾ in. with his fifth jump — and added nearly five inches to that distance with his sixth and final leap.

American Negro, Ralph Boston removed Owens's record from the world list in 1960 with a jump of 26 ft. 11¼ in., and less than a month later also beat Owens's Olympic record when his 26 ft. 7¾ in. won the gold medal in Rome. In May 1961, Boston became the first 27-footer — reaching 27 ft. 0½ in. in May, and 27 ft. 2 in. in June. Then in 1962, Igor Ter-Ovanesian added one and a quarter inches to Boston's record. But two years later, in August 1964, Boston first equalled the Russian's record, and then in September cleared 27 ft. 4¼ in.

Both these world-beaters had to surrender to Great Britain's finest long jumper ever — Lynn Davies, who won the Olympic gold in Tokyo by one and a half inches with a leap of 26 ft. 5¾ in. The three medal-winners from the 1964 Games met again in Mexico City four years later. In the preliminary rounds Boston set up a new Olympic record of 27 ft. 1¾ in., while Bob Beamon, another American Negro, who had cleared 27 ft. 4 in. in July, and Lynn Davies, who had reached exactly 27 ft. in June, qualified for the final only with their third and final leaps.

The final was fantastic. After the first three competitors had fouled their jumps, along came Beamon with a leap of 29 ft. 2½ in., helped by a favourable wind of two metres a second, the maximum allowed for a record. Beamon had beaten the previous world record by 1 ft. 9¾ in. — and had won his gold medal by 2 ft. 4 in. This is one world record which may never be beaten.

Welshman Lynn Davies improved the United Kingdom long jump record from 25 ft. 4½ in. in 1963 to 27 ft. in 1968. He is also the only man to win the Olympic, European and Commonwealth titles.

Max Klauss (GDR). Only seven centimetres separated the first six in the 1971 European championship, Klauss beating former world record-holder Ter-Ovanesian (USSR) by one centimetre

Ralph Boston (USA), 1960 Olympic champion, 1964 silver medallist and 1968 bronze medallist, also the first man to clear 27 ft.

Having qualified for the final at Mexico with the last of three attempts, America's Bob Beamon sailed into the stratosphere with his first jump of 8·90 metres (29 ft. 2½ in.) in the competition proper and added 55 centimetres (21¾ in.) to the previous world record. The new record may well see out the twentieth century. The electric scoreboard (facing page) records Beamon's fantastic win by the competition margin of 71 centimetres (28 in.), easily the biggest margin ever

LONG JUMP · OLYMPIC CHAMPIONS

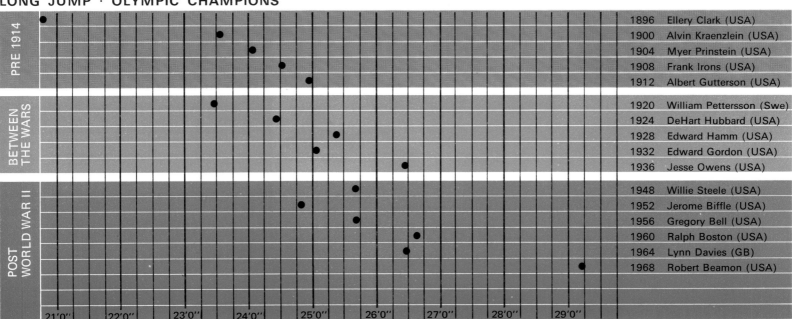

PRE 1914	1896	Ellery Clark (USA)
	1900	Alvin Kraenzlein (USA)
	1904	Myer Prinstein (USA)
	1908	Frank Irons (USA)
	1912	Albert Gutterson (USA)
BETWEEN THE WARS	1920	William Pettersson (Swe)
	1924	DeHart Hubbard (USA)
	1928	Edward Hamm (USA)
	1932	Edward Gordon (USA)
	1936	Jesse Owens (USA)
POST WORLD WAR II	1948	Willie Steele (USA)
	1952	Jerome Biffle (USA)
	1956	Gregory Bell (USA)
	1960	Ralph Boston (USA)
	1964	Lynn Davies (GB)
	1968	Robert Beamon (USA)

21'0'' 22'0'' 23'0'' 24'0'' 25'0'' 26'0'' 27'0'' 28'0'' 29'0''

Triple Jump

This event was originally called the "hop, step and jump", a good description since the competitor must first land on the foot from which he took off (the "hop"), then land on the opposite foot (the "step") and finally on both feet like a long leaper. It was included in the 1896 Games when the winner, James Connolly, an Irish-American, became the first modern Olympic champion, since this was the opening event of the programme.

The Americans included the event in their championships for two years — 1893 and 1894 — and then abandoned it for more than twenty years. It has never featured in American intercollegiate competitions and was not introduced into British championships until 1914.

The Olympic champion in 1900 and 1904 was Myer Prinstein, with over 47 ft. on each occasion. Then in 1908, Timothy Ahearne, an Irishman representing Great Britain, got within three-quarters of an inch of 49 ft. Tim's brother, Dan, who emigrated to America, won the American title eight times between 1910 and 1918 and jumped 50 ft. 11 in. in 1911.

In the 1912 Olympics, Scandinavian competitors took five out of six places, the winner Gustaf Lindblom (Sweden) reaching 48 ft. 5 in. There were some poor performances over the next twelve years, but in the 1924 Olympics, Anthony Winter, of Australia, won with a new world record, just a quarter of an inch better than Ahearne's. A Japanese, Mikio Oda, was sixth.

Four years later, Oda won the Olympic title, and Japan continued to dominate the event in 1932 and 1936, on each occasion with world records. In 1932, Chuhei Nambu raised the world best to 51 ft. 7 in., and four years later Naoto Tajima became the first man to beat 52 ft. Tajima's 52 ft. 6 in. beat Australian Jack Metcalfe's eight-month-old record by nine inches.

In 1950 Adhemar F. da Silva, from Brazil, equalled Tajima's record, and a year later added a quarter of an inch. In the Helsinki Olympics, he raised the world record to 52 ft. 10¾ in. with his second jump, and with his fifth leaped 53 ft. 2½ in.

The following July, Leonid Shcherbakov of Russia, added one centimetre to da Silva's record, but in 1955 da Silva retaliated with the first jump over 54 ft. — and retained his Olympic title in 1956 with a new Olympic record of 53 ft. 7¾ in. In 1958 and 1959, two Russians, Olyeg Ryakhovsky and Olyeg Fedoseyev, cleared 54 ft. 5¼ in. and 54 ft. 9½ in. respectively for new world records, but neither competed in the 1960 Rome Olympics. It was a Pole, Jozef Schmidt, who a month before the Games had raised the world record by over a foot to 55 ft. 10½ in., who won the title with a new Olympic record of 55 ft. 1¾ in. His "hop" measured 19 ft. 7¾ in., the "step" 16 ft. 1 in., and the "jump" 19 ft. 5 in. Schmidt retained his title in Tokyo, again with a new Olympic record of 55 ft. 3½ in., some eleven inches ahead of former world record-holder Olyeg Fedoseyev.

In the 1968 Mexico Games ideal conditions for jumping produced five world records. In the preliminary round, Giuseppe Gentile reached 56 ft. 1¼ in. and followed this with a first jump of 56 ft. 6 in. in the competition proper. About twenty minutes later, Victor Saneyev, U.S.S.R., added one centimetre to the Italian's record — and then Nelson Prudencio from Brazil, improved it by another one and three-quarter inches. Nothing daunted with his final jump, Saneyev cleared 57 ft. 0¾ in. During this fantastic competition, the previous Olympic record of 55 ft. 3½ in. was beaten no less than twelve times. Saneyev's best performance before the Games was 55 ft. 4¼ in., so he showed an improvement of more than twenty inches. Prudencio's improvement was nearly three feet and Gentile's eighteen inches.

Great Britain's best performer in the triple jump has been Fred Alsop, who in 1964 cleared 54 ft. in Tokyo to win fourth place in the Games. Only one other U.K. athlete, Derek Boosey, has exceeded the qualifying distance for Munich Olympics — 53 ft. 1¾ in.

Top: English-born Phil May (now of Australia) won the 1970 Commonwealth title by a foot with a jump of 54 ft. 10 in. He also finished second to Lynn Davies in the long jump. Above: Jozef Schmidt of Poland. His world record of 55 ft. 10½ in., set up in 1960, stood for eight years, until it was broken eight times in the more favourable atmosphere of Mexico. Schmidt was twice Olympic (1960 and 1964) and twice European (1958 and 1962) champion

Victor Saneyev (USSR), Olympic champion in 1968 with a new world record of 57 ft. 0¾ in. — the first man to beat 57 ft. He qualified for the final with a modest 53 ft. 2¾ in., while the Italian

Giuseppe Gentile had himself achieved a world record of 56 ft. 1¼ in. Then in the competition proper, Gentile with his first jump reached 56 ft. 6 in., while Saneyev took the lead in the third

round with a quarter-inch more. In the fifth round, the Brazilian Nelson Prudencio reached 56 ft. 8 in., but with his final jump the Russian clinched the "gold" with nearly five inches to spare

TRIPLE JUMP · OLYMPIC CHAMPIONS

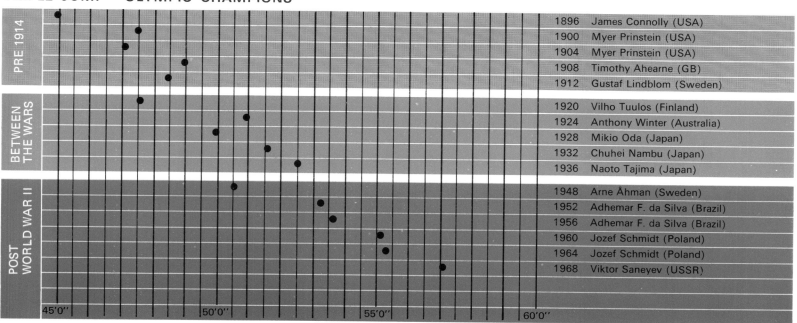

PRE 1914	1896	James Connolly (USA)
	1900	Myer Prinstein (USA)
	1904	Myer Prinstein (USA)
	1908	Timothy Ahearne (GB)
	1912	Gustaf Lindblom (Sweden)
BETWEEN THE WARS	1920	Vilho Tuulos (Finland)
	1924	Anthony Winter (Australia)
	1928	Mikio Oda (Japan)
	1932	Chuhei Nambu (Japan)
	1936	Naoto Tajima (Japan)
POST WORLD WAR II	1948	Arne Åhman (Sweden)
	1952	Adhemar F. da Silva (Brazil)
	1956	Adhemar F. da Silva (Brazil)
	1960	Jozef Schmidt (Poland)
	1964	Jozef Schmidt (Poland)
	1968	Viktor Saneyev (USSR)

45'0"   50'0"   55'0"   60'0"

Putting the Shot

In 1965, Randy Matson (USA) added nearly three feet to the world record with a prodigious throw of 70 ft. 7¼ in. Two years later he reached 71 ft. 5½ in. Matson won the Olympic title in Mexico with 67 ft. 4¾ in., having set up a new Olympic record of 67 ft. 10¼ in. in the qualifying round. American athletes have held the world record for thirty-eight years, during which time it has improved by over seventeen feet

In England, this event was originally known as putting-the-weight, though "shot-putting" has been the term always used in the United States. Shot-putting is now universally accepted, and is probably the more accurate, since the event was introduced into sport through soldiers using cannon balls.

The weight of the shot is 16 lb., and the event has featured in competitions since the middle of the nineteenth century. Until 1908, the athlete operated from a 7 ft. square — the 7 ft. circle being introduced in the Olympics of that year. On fifteen of sixteen occasions, the Olympic gold medal has been won by an American, and the United States can claim a total of thirty-five medals out of a possible forty-eight. The only non-American gold medallist was a German, Hans Wöllke, who on the first day of the Berlin Games became the first athlete ever to win a gold medal for Germany.

The first outstanding shot-putter was Ralph Rose of the U.S.A., who was the Olympic champion in 1904 and 1908, and silver medallist in 1912. His world record in 1909 of exactly 51 ft., stood for over eighteen years. It was beaten by a German, Emil Hirschfeld, with 51 ft. 9¾ in., some eight weeks before the 1928 Olympics. But at Amsterdam, the winner was American, Johnny Kuck, who won with a world record of just over 52 ft., and this was the last time a world record for this event was achieved in the Olympics.

In 1953, Parry O'Brien, who won the gold medal at the Helsinki Olympics by less than one inch with a putt of 57 ft. 1½ in., set up a new world record, and in May 1956, became the first man to exceed 61 ft. Four weeks before the Melbourne Games, he raised the world record to over 63 ft., and though he could not get within a couple of feet of this distance at Melbourne, he retained his Olympic title with a new record for the Games of 60 ft. 11¼ in.

In 1960 in Rome, O'Brien was faced by two other Americans, Bill Nieder and Dallas Long, each of whom earlier in the year had beaten his world record. Nieder beat O'Brien with two feet to spare and Long, four inches behind O'Brien, gained the bronze medal.

In July 1964, Long raised the world record to 67 ft. 10 in., and at the Tokyo Olympics won the gold with 66 ft. 8½ in. Five inches behind was Randy Matson, destined three years later to reach the remarkable distance of 71 ft. 5¼ in. In fourth place was the evergreen O'Brien, taking part in his fourth Olympics, and recording his best effort, so far as Olympics were concerned, of 63 ft. exactly. Two years later he reached 64 ft. 7¼ in., but by that time the world record was over 70 ft.

The 1968 Games victor was Randy Matson, with an effort four feet short of his world record, but a foot further than any other competitor.

So far as the British Isles are concerned, Ireland as part of the U.K. until 1922, has produced some fine exponents. Many of them competed for the U.S.A., including Dennis Horgan who gained a silver medal in 1908 with a very modest 44 ft. 8 in. In 1904, he had putt 48 ft. 10 in., then a world best. In 1961, Arthur Rowe became the best-ever British performer with 64 ft. 2 in. Geoffrey Capes, our leader at the start of the seventies, may soon exceed this distance. But, throughout the world in 1971, ten athletes had beaten 66 ft. 6 in.

Right: Arthur Rowe (GB), 1958 European champion (58 ft. 4 in.) and Commonwealth champion (57 ft. 8 in.). In five years Rowe increased the United Kingdom record from 55 ft. 6 in. to 64 ft. 2 in. in twelve stages

Far right: From 1953 to 1959, Parry O'Brien (USA) held the world record, becoming the first man to beat 59, 60, 61, 62 and 63 ft. He won the Olympic title in 1952 and retained it four years later. But in 1960 he had to surrender to fellow American Dallas Long

Twenty-two-year-old Hartmut Briesenick (GDR) beat fellow German Hans-Joachim Rothenburg by two feet with a new European record of 69 ft. 2 in., which Rothenburg was soon to beat by another inch and a half. These two should offer serious opposition to the Americans at Munich

Retaining his Commonwealth title in Edinburgh, David Steen (Can) also improved his Games record of 61 ft. 8 in. by over a foot. Les Mills of New Zealand, Commonwealth record-holder with 64 ft. 11¾ in., was third

PUTTING THE SHOT · OLYMPIC CHAMPIONS

PRE 1914		1896	Robert Garrett (USA)
		1900	Richard Sheldon (USA)
		1904	Ralph Rose (USA)
		1908	Ralph Rose (USA)
		1912	Patrick McDonald (USA)
BETWEEN THE WARS		1920	Ville Pörhölä (Finland)
		1924	Clarence Houser (USA)
		1928	John Kuck (USA)
		1932	Leo Sexton (USA)
		1936	Hans Wöllke (Germany)
POST WORLD WAR II		1948	Wilbur Thompson (USA)
		1952	Parry O'Brien (USA)
		1956	Parry O'Brien (USA)
		1960	William Nieder (USA)
		1964	Dallas Long (USA)
		1968	Randy Matson (USA)

40'0" 45'0" 50'0" 55'0" 60'0" 65'0" 70'0"

Throwing the Discus

The discus, originating in Ancient Greece, was one of the five events in the Greek all-round competition – the pentathlon. One of the most famous statues in the world is "The Discobolous" (discus thrower) by Myron, but the discus in use then was bigger and heavier than the modern one. Today's discus weighs 2 kilograms (4 lb. 6½ oz.) and has a diameter of 8¾ in. It is thrown from a circle 2·50 metres (8 ft. 2½ in.) in diameter.

The discus was one of the two throwing events included in the 1896 Olympic programme. Much to the chagrin of the Greeks, the American Robert Garrett, who had never competed in the event before, beat the Greek champion, Athanasics Paraskevopoulos, by seven and three-quarter inches. Garrett later also won the shot. It should, in fairness, be added that the Greeks were much more concerned with showing graceful form than throwing long distances.

Four years later, amid the trees of the Bois de Boulogne in Paris, a Hungarian won the title. The first six throwers all beat 100 ft. and Paraskevopoulos improved his Athens effort of 95 ft. to 111 ft. 8 in.

Martin Sheridan of America repeated his 1904 Games victory with a gold medal in 1908, when Americans finished first, second and third. Sheridan also won the discus thrown "Greek style" from a platform, the only time this event gained Olympic status. Americans have also taken all three medals on two other occasions – 1956 and 1960 – and, with twelve gold medals, have won a total of thirty medals out of a possible forty-eight.

From the VIIIth Olympiad in 1924, to the XIXth in Mexico forty-four years later, the American run of successes has been broken only once. That was in 1948, when the great Italian exponent, Adolfo Consolini, beat his national rival Giuseppe Tosi by over three feet with a new Olympic record of 173 ft. 2 in. At every subsequent Games, the record has been bettered. In 1956 in Melbourne, American Al Oerter, just out of his teens, reached a new Olympic record of 184 ft. 10½ in. to gain the first of his four consecutive gold medals for the event.

In 1964, Oerter exceeded 200 ft. by one and a half inches, beating Ludvik Danek, the

In 1956, with his first throw, Al Oerter (USA) set up a new Olympic record of 184 ft. 10 in., and won his first Olympic gold medal. Three times more, in 1960, 1964 and 1968, he repeated these successes, and in 1968 raised the record to 212 ft. 6 in. No one else has won an Olympic title four times. Oerter was also the first man to exceed 200 ft. with the discus.

Czechoslovakian world record-holder and 1971 European champion, by eighteen inches.

By 1968, 200 ft. was becoming rather commonplace, the world record being held by another American, Jay Silvester, who two months before the Games had thrown 224 ft. 5 in. In the qualifying round Silvester led the field with a new Olympic best of 207 ft. 10 in. But in the final, Oerter reached 212 ft. 6 in. — and Silvester had to be content with fifth place with 202 ft. 8 in.

In 1971 thirty men threw over 202 ft.

The discus was not introduced into the British Championships until 1914. Mark Pharaoh, the only Englishman to finish in the first six in the Olympics since 1896, with a national record of 178 ft. in 1956, was the first outstanding U.K. performer. Since then, Gerald Carr, Mike Lindsay, Bill Tancred and John Watts, the present record-holder, have thrown further than Pharaoh.

Left: Ludvik Danek (Cze), winner of the 1971 European title with a throw of 209 ft. 8 in. He was also the first man to beat 210 ft. when he established a new world record of 211 ft. 9 in. in 1964, and his best throw has been 218 ft. 2 in.

Latvian-born George Puce (Can) wrested the 1970 Commonwealth title from Les Mills of New Zealand, whom he beat by nearly four feet with a new Games record of 193 ft. 7 in. In 1968 he set up a Commonwealth record of 211 ft. 3 in.

THROWING THE DISCUS · OLYMPIC CHAMPIONS

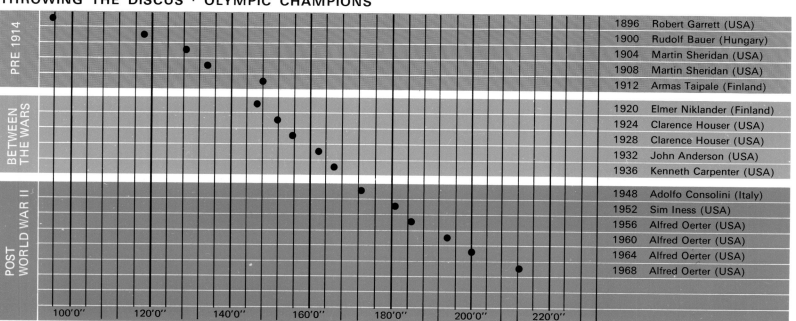

1896	Robert Garrett (USA)
1900	Rudolf Bauer (Hungary)
1904	Martin Sheridan (USA)
1908	Martin Sheridan (USA)
1912	Armas Taipale (Finland)
1920	Elmer Niklander (Finland)
1924	Clarence Houser (USA)
1928	Clarence Houser (USA)
1932	John Anderson (USA)
1936	Kenneth Carpenter (USA)
1948	Adolfo Consolini (Italy)
1952	Sim Iness (USA)
1956	Alfred Oerter (USA)
1960	Alfred Oerter (USA)
1964	Alfred Oerter (USA)
1968	Alfred Oerter (USA)

100'0"   120'0"   140'0"   160'0"   180'0"   200'0"   220'0"

Throwing the Hammer

The modern "hammer" is a metal ball on a swivel connected to a length of steel wire, and weighs 16 lb. It is the successor to the sledge-hammer which was thrown in England since the sixteenth century, and there are prints of Henry VIII throwing something similar to a blacksmith's hammer. In the earliest days, the distance thrown was measured from the position of the feet as the hammer was released. Then, a scratch line was used for measuring, and later this became a 7 ft. or 9 ft. circle. Today, the circle is 7 ft., and for a throw to be valid it must fall within a sector of 45 degrees.

The hammer was first included in the 1900 Olympic Games, and was won by one of the many great Irish-American hammer-throwers — John Flanagan. He repeated his success at the next two Games. It was in 1928 that Patrick O'Callaghan, perhaps the greatest Irish athlete of them all, won the first Olympic title for the independent Irish State, and in 1932 he took his second gold medal in Los Angeles.

In 1936, the Americans were not in the first three. With his second throw, before a wildly excited home crowd, German Erwin Blask beat the twenty-four-year-old Olympic record by exactly a foot. And another German, Karl Hein, won the Games title with a final throw of 185 ft. 4 in. Two years later, Blask beat Ryan's world record.

In the first post-war Olympics, it was a Hungarian, Imre Németh, who won the title and raised the Olympic record to 197 ft. 11½ in. He led the first five competitors, who all beat the previous Olympic record.

The Olympic title returned to the United States in 1956 — their first victory for over thirty years. The field included Sverre Strandli, of Norway, who four years earlier had become the first man to beat 200 ft., Mikhail Krivonosov of the U.S.S.R. who, in October, had raised the world record to 220 ft. 10 in., József Csermák the reigning champion, and Harold Connolly, who in early November had added four feet to Krivonosov's world record. With four rounds completed, Krivonosov, with 206 ft. 9 in., was over a foot ahead of Connolly, but the American won the title by six inches with his fifth throw.

Connolly, who in 1960 became the first hammer-thrower to exceed 230 ft., competed in three more Olympics — but he never again was among the medallists.

Russia gained her first hammer victory in the 1960 Rome Games, a success she repeated in 1964, and on each occasion, the Hungarian Gyula Zsivotzky was second. At his third Olympic attempt in Mexico, Zsivotzky, who in 1965 had become the first man to exceed 240 ft., won the gold medal by three inches from the 1964 champion, Romuald Klim, of the U.S.S.R. The first ten competitors beat 220 ft.

Great Britain's first 200-footer was Mike Ellis, who in 1959 threw 213 ft. 1 in. Howard Payne, who was born in South Africa, captured the United Kingdom national record with 227 ft. 2 in. This performance ranked him number twenty in the 1970 world list.

Silver medallist in 1960 and again in 1964, it was third time lucky for Gyula Zsivotzky of Hungary when in 1968 he won the "gold" with three inches to spare over the reigning Olympic champion Romuald Klim (USSR). A month before the Games Zsivotzky had also established a world record of 242 ft. He was European champion in 1962

In 1970, Howard Payne of Great Britain won his third "gold" in the Commonwealth Games, and set up a Games record of 222 ft. 5 in. He was thus the first male athlete to accomplish a triple victory in any event. He threw 223 ft. 3 in. at the Mexico Olympics

THROWING THE HAMMER · OLYMPIC CHAMPIONS

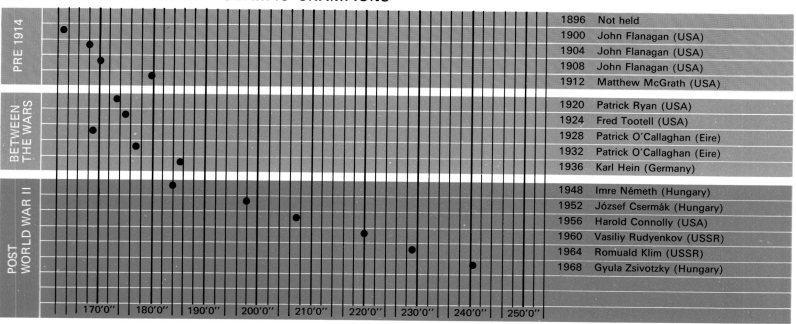

PRE 1914	1896	Not held
	1900	John Flanagan (USA)
	1904	John Flanagan (USA)
	1908	John Flanagan (USA)
	1912	Matthew McGrath (USA)
BETWEEN THE WARS	1920	Patrick Ryan (USA)
	1924	Fred Tootell (USA)
	1928	Patrick O'Callaghan (Eire)
	1932	Patrick O'Callaghan (Eire)
	1936	Karl Hein (Germany)
POST WORLD WAR II	1948	Imre Németh (Hungary)
	1952	József Csermák (Hungary)
	1956	Harold Connolly (USA)
	1960	Vasiliy Rudyenkov (USSR)
	1964	Romuald Klim (USSR)
	1968	Gyula Zsivotzky (Hungary)

170'0" 180'0" 190'0" 200'0" 210'0" 220'0" 230'0" 240'0" 250'0"

Throwing the Javelin

The javelin, so useful in war and in hunting, was practised as a sport in Ancient Greece, and was, in fact, one of the five events in the original pentathlon. As far as England is concerned, there were early javelin contests for accuracy, not distance. It was the Scandinavians who encouraged and developed javelin competitions for distance.

The javelin was included in the modern Olympic Games for the first time in 1908, when there were two competitions. One was with the javelin held in the middle, which is the modern method, and the other termed "freestyle", in which you held it where you pleased. The modern javelin for men weighs 800 grammes (1 lb. 12 oz.) and is over 8 ft. 6 in. long.

In the 1908 Olympic event, the first six places went to Scandinavians, the winner being Erik Lemming of Sweden. In the 1912 Games in Stockholm, eleven of the twelve places were occupied by Scandinavians, the only exception being Mór Koczán, of Hungary, who won the bronze medal. In the first four Olympics after the first world war, Scandinavians held sway. The greatest performer was Matti Järvinen, who won the Olympic title in 1932 with a throw of 238 ft. 6½ in., a feat which is permanently recorded as the height of the Marathon Tower in the Olympic Stadium at Helsinki.

Over a period of six years, Järvinen, whose father competed in the 1908 Games and whose three brothers were all fine athletes, raised the world record ten times to a final distance of 253 ft. 4 in. less than two months before the Berlin Games.

Järvinen defended his Olympic title in Berlin, but was seriously handicapped by a back injury. He finished sixth, nearly nine feet below the winner, Gerhard Stöck of Germany. Järvinen's throw was twenty-five feet below his best.

In 1952, the U.S.A. gained their only javelin Olympic victory when Cyrus Young set up a new Games record of 242 ft. Four years later Young lead the qualifiers with 242 ft. 5 in., but could only produce a throw of 222 ft. in the competition proper, to finish eleventh. The winner, Egil Danielsen of Norway, produced a then fantastic throw of 281 ft. 2 in., over nineteen feet ahead of Janusz Sidlo, of Poland, whose world record had stood at 274 ft. 5 in. since the previous June. Danielsen's Olympic record remained until 1968 when it was beaten by the three medallists.

By the early seventies five men had thrown 300 ft.

Apart from the Americans Bud Held, inventor of the famous "Held aerodynamic javelin", and Al Cantello, the Italian Carlo Lievore, and Janis Lusis of the U.S.S.R., the world record has always been in Scandinavian hands.

Few U.K. athletes have seriously pursued this event, 220 ft. not being reached by a performer till 1952, by which date the world record was forty feet more. David Travis the 1970 Commonwealth champion who represented Great Britain in the Mexico Olympics, captured the record with 273 ft. 9 in., and this ranked him eighteenth in the world.

Janis Lusis (USSR), four times European champion, and 1968 Olympic gold medallist, former world record-holder, and the second man to throw the javelin over 300 ft.

Second to Lusis in Mexico, Jorma Kinnunen of Finland deprived the Russian of the world record

the following year by adding two feet four inches with a throw of 304 ft. 1 in.

After thirty years nearly fifty feet has been added to the world record.

At Melbourne, Egil Danielsen of Norway suddenly added over forty feet to his previous best in the competition and leapt from sixth to first place for an Olympic title and a world record

Britain's David Travis won the "gold" at the 1970 Commonwealth Games with a throw of 260 ft. 10 in. Four weeks later he set up a new British and Commonwealth record of 273 ft. 9 in.

THROWING THE JAVELIN · OLYMPIC CHAMPIONS

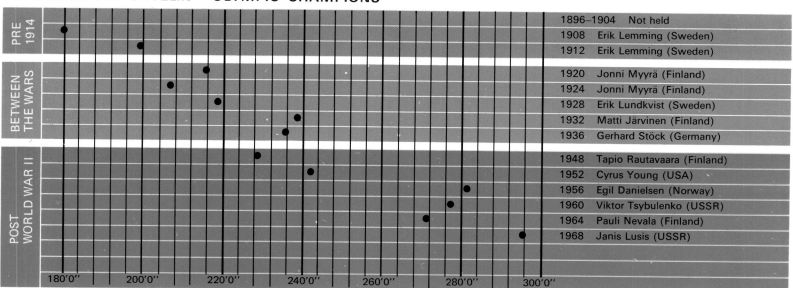

PRE 1914	1896–1904 Not held
	1908 Erik Lemming (Sweden)
	1912 Erik Lemming (Sweden)
BETWEEN THE WARS	1920 Jonni Myyrä (Finland)
	1924 Jonni Myyrä (Finland)
	1928 Erik Lundkvist (Sweden)
	1932 Matti Järvinen (Finland)
	1936 Gerhard Stöck (Germany)
POST WORLD WAR II	1948 Tapio Rautavaara (Finland)
	1952 Cyrus Young (USA)
	1956 Egil Danielsen (Norway)
	1960 Viktor Tsybulenko (USSR)
	1964 Pauli Nevala (Finland)
	1968 Janis Lusis (USSR)

180'0"   200'0"   220'0"   240'0"   260'0"   280'0"   300'0"

Women's Events

International women's athletics celebrated its jubilee in 1971, fifty years after female representatives from five nations had taken part in the "Monte Carlo" Games of 1921, and an unofficial match between England and France held later in the same year. The Fédération Sportive Féminine Internationale was formed in October 1921, and this organisation was responsible for international women's athletics until 1936 when, after the Berlin Olympics, it was replaced by the International Amateur Athletic Federation.

Women's events were first included in the 1928 Olympic Games in Amsterdam. The F.S.F.I., who had held a one-day "World Games" in Paris in 1922, which attracted a crowd of 20,000, had their application for the admission of female athletes to the 1924 Games refused. So they staged a second "Women's World Games" in Gothenburg in 1926, and two others took place in Prague in 1930 and in London in 1934.

The London meeting consisted of the 60, 100, 200 and 800 metres, 400 metres relay and 80 metres hurdles, together with the high jump, long jump, shot, discus, javelin and pentathlon. Barriers to female athletes were being gradually broken down, and events for them were included in the British Empire Games in 1934 and a special Women's European Games was staged in Vienna in 1938.

The acceptance of a full Olympic programme for women became a gradual process. In 1928, there were only five events — the 100 and 800 metres, 4×100 metres relay, high jump and discus. The 800 metres was dropped from the 1932 programme, and the 80 metres hurdles and javelin added. Then, in 1948, the 200 metres, long jump and shot putt were added, and after an interval of thirty-two years, the 800 metres was reinstated in the 1960 Olympics.

The 400 metres and pentathlon were included in 1964, and at the Munich Games the 4×400 metres relay and the 1,500 metres are to be included. Both these last two events for women were held in the 1969 and 1971 European Championships.

So far as recognition of world records for women is concerned, the 400 metres and 440 yards were first recognised in 1957, the 1,500 metres and one mile ten years later and the 3,000 metres in 1970. The 4×400 metres and 4×400 yards relays were added to the list in 1968, when the 4×800 metres and 4×880 yards relays were substituted for the 3×800 metres and 3×880 yards relays.

Facing page, top left: Betty Cuthbert (Aus) captures her fourth Olympic "gold", beating Ann Packer (GB) by one-fifth of a second in the first-ever Olympic women's 400 metres — Tokyo 1964

Facing page, top right: A puzzled Mary Bignal fails to reach the final stages of the long jump at the 1960 Rome Olympics. But four years later, as Mary Rand . . . !

Facing page, bottom: In the 1968 Women's A.A.A. Championships at Crystal Palace, held on the new all-weather track, Vera Nikolic (no. 44) of Yugoslavia, who had won the 1966 European title at the age of eighteen, set up a new world record of 2 min. 0·5 sec. for the 800 metres. Lillian Board was second in her first serious race over the distance

Right: On the same afternoon that her husband Emil Zatopek won the Olympic 5,000 metres title, Dana Zátopková won the javelin and expressed her delight at the twin family victory. For seven weeks in 1958 Dana held the world record of 182 ft. 10 in. until Anna Pazera (Aus) won the Commonwealth event with 188 ft. 4 in.

Women's Track Events

Fanny Blankers-Koen (Neth), mother of two, wins the first women's 200 metres Olympic title in 1948. She earned twelve record plaques for nine different events

Women's organised athletics goes back just about half a century. In March 1921 a meeting was held in Monte Carlo. There were three individual track events over 60 metres, 250 metres and 800 metres. Mary Lines of Great Britain won the first two, was second in the 800 metres in 2 min. 32·8 sec., and competed in two successful British relay teams. However, it was a somewhat tentative experiment, and though women's events were included in the 1928 Olympics, women athletes did not really come into their own until the second world war. To give some idea of the improvement in performances, I give the world records for Olympic events in 1936 and at the end of 1971:

		1936		1971	percentage improvement
metres	min.	sec.	min.	sec.	
100		11·7		11·0	6%
200		23·6		22·4	5
400		56·6		51·0	9
800	2	16·8	1	58·5	13
4×100 relay		46·4		42·8	8

I have not included the 80 metres hurdles (since this event is now over 100 metres), nor the 1,500 metres and 4×400 metres relay, since these two events are included in this year's Olympic Games for the first time.

The following athletes have been placed in the first three in two or more Olympics:

100 metres: Stella Walsh (1st, 1932; 2nd, 1936), Wyomia Tyus (1st, 1964; 1st, 1968), Shirley Strickland (2nd, 1948; 3rd, 1952)

200 metres: Irena Kirszenstein (2nd, 1964; 1st, 1968)

80 metres hurdles: Shirley Strickland (3rd, 1948; 1st, 1952; 1st, 1956), Pam Kilborn (3rd, 1964; 2nd, 1968)

Here are some of my outstanding recollections of Olympics women's track events.

1932 Los Angeles
Stella Walsh (or to give her Polish name, Stanislawa Walasiewicz) won the 100 metres, recording 11·9 sec. three times. Two years later she was to set up a world record of 11·7 sec. Mildred Didrikson won the 80 metres hurdles.

1936 Berlin
Helen Stephens beat Stella Walsh in the 100 metres, and also "anchored" the American relay team to victory in 46·9 sec. In this relay, the German team, having set up a new world record of 46·4 sec., and in possession of a decisive lead, dropped the baton in the final.

1948 London
Undoubtedly Fanny Blankers-Koen, who won the "gold" in the three track events and the hurdles, was the outstanding performer.

1952 Helsinki
Marjorie Jackson of Australia won a brilliant "double", equalling the world record in the 100 metres and setting up a new world best in the 200 metres. With Marjorie as "anchor" woman in the sprint relay, the Australian team set up a new world record in the heats. However, in the final, the baton was knocked out of her hand, and though it bounced and she caught it, valuable fractions of a second were lost and the team finished fifth. Another Australian, Shirley Strickland, won the hurdles.

1956 Melbourne
More Australian sprinters. Betty Cuthbert won both sprints and "anchored" the relay team which beat Great Britain by a yard in the new world record time of 44·5 sec. Shirley Strickland repeated her success in the hurdles.

1960 Rome
Wilma Rudolph, who had become the first woman to beat 23·0 sec. for the 200 metres, also became the first coloured woman to win an Olympic sprint title. In the sprint relay she "anchored" the American team to another world record. Some ten months later she set up a new 100 metres record of 11·2 sec. Dorothy Hyman was a fine second in the 100 metres and third in the 200 metres. The reinstated 800 metres was won by Lyudmila Shevtsova (U.S.S.R.) who equalled her two-month-old world record of 2 min. 04·3 sec.

1964 Tokyo
Wyomia Tyus proved a worthy successor to Wilma Rudolph in the 100 metres, while the 200 metres went to another American negress, Edith Maguire. Irena Kirszenstein (Poland) was second in the 200 metres and a member of the successful Polish sprint relay team which set up a new world record of 43·6 sec. Subsequently, however, the eligibility of one of the Polish team was questioned. The team kept the Olympic title, but their record was removed from the books.

The new 400 metres event produced a fine win for Betty Cuthbert, while Ann Packer of Great Britain, who finished second in the 400 metres, secured what was perhaps the outstanding woman's victory of the Games in the 800 metres in the world record time of 2 min. 01·1 sec.

1968 Mexico
Wyomia Tyus retained her 100 metres title (the first ever to do so), reached the final of the 200 metres and "anchored" the U.S.A. world record quartet in the relay.

Lillian Board just lost the 400 metres to Colette Besson of France, while Madeline Manning won the 800 metres by more than twelve yards in the new Olympic record time of 2 min. 00·9 sec. Irena Szewinska (Kirszenstein) set up a new world record in winning the 200 metres.

Australia won the 80 metres hurdles (the last time this event was to be held) in another Olympic record of 10·3 sec.

Colette Besson congratulates Lillian Board after her victory in the 1969 Great Britain v. France match. The previous year, in Mexico, the placings had been reversed.

100 Metres

The very first woman Olympic track and field gold medallist was Elizabeth Robinson, of the United States who, on the afternoon of July 31st, 1928, won the 100 metres in 12·2 sec. A year earlier, Miss Robinson had set up a new world best of 12·2 sec., and on June 2nd, 1928, had reduced this to 12·0 sec. Myrtle Cook of Canada equalled it a month later.

Miss Cook, naturally thought to be Miss Robinson's most serious rival, reached the final of the 1928 Games 100 metres but, along with Hermine Schmidt, of Germany, was disqualified for more than two false starts.

Four years later, in June 1932, Tollina Schuurman, of the Netherlands, became the first woman to beat 12·0 sec. with 11·9 sec. However, Miss Schuurman did not reach the final of the Olympic 100 metres in Los Angeles, which was won by Poland's Stanislawa Walasiewicz, perhaps better known as Stella Walsh. Although she was born in Poland, Stella Walsh was educated in the United States, and later became an American citizen. She was one of the most remarkable women athletes of all time, winning more than forty American titles, indoors and out, from sprinting to long jumping and the discus. In October 1934, Miss Walsh reduced the world 100 metres record to 11·7 sec. She defended her Olympic title in 1936, but had to surrender to Helen Stephens, of the U.S.A. A few days after the Games, in Dresden, Miss Stephens returned an 11·5 sec., which was not recognised as a world record.

In 1937 Stella Walsh returned 11·6 sec — a time beaten in 1948 by Fanny Blankers-Koen, who was the outstanding performer at the Games in London, where she won the 100 and 200 metres, 80 metres hurdles and anchored the Netherlands team in the sprint relay.

The era of American negress successes opened in Rome in 1960 with Wilma Rudolph. Wilma, at the age of four had suffered from paralysis of the left leg. Yet, at the age of sixteen she had been a member of the U.S.A. sprint relay team which gained the bronze medal in Melbourne in 1956. After equalling the Olympic record of 11·5 sec. in her Rome heat, she set up a new world record of 11·3 sec. in her semi-final and then won the final in 11·0 sec. with a following wind which was 0·75 metre per second over the limit.

Second to Wilma, who in 1961 became the first woman to do 11·2 sec., was Dorothy Hyman of Great Britain. She was succeeded by another American negress, Wyomia Tyus, who in Tokyo 1964, did 11·2 sec. to equal the world record in her second-round heat. In

1968, Wyomia successfully defended her title, becoming the first woman to do so in the 100 metres. Equalling the Olympic record of 11·2 sec. in her heat, she did 11·0 sec. in the second round, but with a favourable wind of 2·7 m.p.h. In the final she did a world record of 11·0 sec.

Below left: Dorothy Hyman, surely Britain's greatest woman sprinter, with two Commonwealth individual gold medals and one European at the top of her remarkable list of achievements
Below right: Chi Cheng (Tai), the first woman to run 100 yards in even time. She has also held world records at 100 metres, 200 metres, 220 yards and 100 metres hurdles

Wyomia Tyus (USA), the first athlete, man or woman, ever to retain an Olympic 100 metres title. She won in 1964 and 1968, and also anchored the victorious American relay team in 1968

100 METRES · OLYMPIC CHAMPIONS

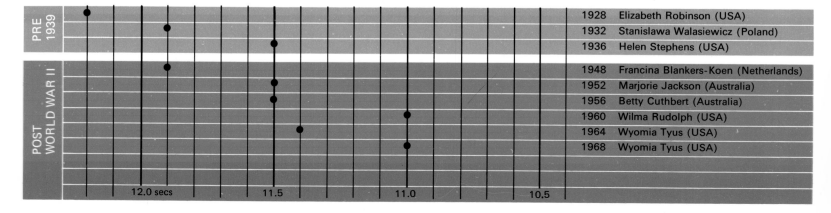

PRE 1939	1928	Elizabeth Robinson (USA)
	1932	Stanislawa Walasiewicz (Poland)
	1936	Helen Stephens (USA)
POST WORLD WAR II	1948	Francina Blankers-Koen (Netherlands)
	1952	Marjorie Jackson (Australia)
	1956	Betty Cuthbert (Australia)
	1960	Wilma Rudolph (USA)
	1964	Wyomia Tyus (USA)
	1968	Wyomia Tyus (USA)

12.0 secs   11.5   11.0   10.5

200 Metres

Though the 220 yards was included in the Second Empire Games, held in London in 1934, it was not until 1948 that the 200 metres was included in the Olympic Games. As early as 1935, Stella Walsh had set up a world record of 23·6 sec. for the 200 metres, a time not beaten for seventeen years. In 1948, Fanny Blankers-Koen, then thirty years of age and a mother of two, easily captured the 200 metres in 24·3 sec.

Two years later, Fanny set up a new world record of 24·2 sec. for the 220 yards, bringing her total number of individual world record plaques to eight. In 1951, she added the pentathlon to this total, at the age of thirty-three.' Since retiring, she has often acted as coach and manager to the Netherlands women's teams.

In Helsinki 1952, Marjorie Jackson equalled the world record of 23·6 sec. in her heat, and set up a new world record of 23·4 sec. in the semi-final. In the final, she won in 23·7 sec. Marjorie retained both her Commonwealth sprint titles in 1954, but did not compete in the 1956 Olympics, the event being won by a fellow Australian, Betty Cuthbert, who equalled the Olympic record of 23·4 sec. This was one-fifth of a second slower than the world record she had created in Sydney a couple of months before the Melbourne Games.

In 1960 the 200 metres Olympic title went to the American negress, Wilma Rudolph who, during July, had reduced the world record to 22·9 sec. to become the first woman to beat 23·0 sec. She had no difficulty in winning the final after setting up a new Olympic record in her heat of 23·2 sec.

The success of the American negresses was repeated in 1964 in Tokyo, when Edith McGuire recorded a narrow win over Irena Kirszenstein of Poland, in the final. Four years later in Mexico, the Pole, who had created a world record of 22·7 sec. in 1965, won in the new world record time of 22·5 sec., with a wind of exactly 2 metres per second.

Britain's best performer at the time of writing is Dorothy Hyman, dual Commonwealth champion in 1962, European 100 metres gold medallist, and silver medallist in the 200 metres.

Above: Renate Stecher (GDR) — formerly Meissner — 1971 dual European gold medallist in the 100 and 200 metres, and joint world record-holder for the 100 metres

Right: Irena Szewinska (formerly Kirszenstein) of Poland, member of the victorious Polish relay team in the 1964 Olympics and winner of the 200 metres in 1968 in the new world record time of 22·5 sec.

200 METRES · OLYMPIC CHAMPIONS

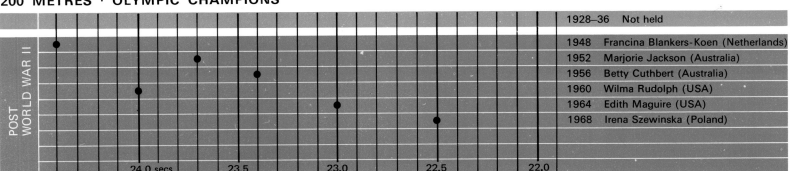

POST WORLD WAR II		
1928–36	Not held	
1948	Francina Blankers-Koen (Netherlands)	
1952	Marjorie Jackson (Australia)	
1956	Betty Cuthbert (Australia)	
1960	Wilma Rudolph (USA)	
1964	Edith Maguire (USA)	
1968	Irena Szewinska (Poland)	

24.0 secs   23.5   23.0   22.5   22.0

400 Metres

Below left: Helga Seidler (GDR), 400 metres winner in the 1971 European Championships in 52·1 sec., and a member of the relay team which set up a world record of 3 min. 29·3 sec.
Below right: Marilyn Neufville won the European indoor women's title in 1970 for Great Britain, and captured the Commonwealth title for Jamaica in the world record time of 51·0 sec.

The 400 metres for women was first introduced into the Olympic Games in Tokyo, 1964, though the event had been included in the European Championships in 1958. The 1964 Olympic final included Russian Maria Itkina, the former world record-holder. Great Britain's representative was Ann Packer, who had returned the fastest times in her heat and in the semi-final, as well as Betty Cuthbert, the Australian triple gold medallist in the 1956 Olympics and holder of the world record for 440 yards. The 400 metres world record-holder, Shin Kim Dan of North Korea, had been entered for the event, but her country had withdrawn from the Games at the last moment, for political reasons.

Packer, in lane six, was favourite, but she was a yard down on Cuthbert running in lane one, as the runners entered the finishing straight against a strong wind. Packer could not make any impression on the sturdy Australian, who won in 52·0 sec., and she had to be content with a silver medal and a British record. Third, but a long way back in 53·4 sec., was Judith Amoore who, the following year, was to set up a world record for the 440 yards.

Judith Amoore won the 440 yards Commonwealth 1966 title in Kingston, Jamaica, with a then almost unknown English runner, seventeen-year-old Lillian Board, behind her in fifth place. In 1967, Lillian Board rose to the front of world 400-metre runners, when in July, in Los Angeles, she beat Judith Amoore, who is now Mrs Pollock, in 52·8 sec. This was one second faster than Miss Board had ever run before. She was promptly and, I have always thought most regrettably, made favourite for the Mexico Games which was then over a year away. Board's running in the 1968 preliminary rounds added to the odds that she would win the gold. In the semi-final, she ran her best-ever time of 52·5 sec., the fastest of all the qualifiers.

In the final, she was in lane one, and though tiring visibly and not looking quite at ease, seemed a certain winner with fifty yards to go. Then, almost from nowhere, came Colette Besson, of France, to win in a time equalling the Olympic record of 52·0 sec.

In 1969, Besson lost her European title to a fellow-Frenchwoman, Nicole Duclos, both being given the same new world record of 51·7 sec.

Less than a year later, seventeen-year-old Marilyn Neufville, Jamaican-born but British-trained, and a girl who had won the first European indoor championship in March 1970, won the Commonwealth title by the best part of twenty yards in the new world record time of 51·0 sec.

The 1971 European title went to twenty-two-year-old Helga Seidler, of East Germany, in 52·1 sec. — eight-tenths of a second ahead of Inge Bodding of West Germany. Besson finished seventh.

"Oh, the little less and what worlds away!"
Colette Besson (Fr) beats Lillian Board (GB) by seven-hundredths of a second for the coveted Olympic "gold" in Mexico

400 METRES · OLYMPIC CHAMPIONS

POST WORLD WAR II			
1928–60	Not held		
1964	Betty Cuthbert (Australia)		
1968	Colette Besson (France)		

52.5 secs   52.0   51.5   51.0   50.5   50.0

800 Metres

When women's events were rather grudgingly included in the Olympic track and field programme at Amsterdam in 1928, the 800 metres was one of them. The race was won by Lina Radke, of Germany, in what was the first "officially recognised" world record time of 2 min. 16·8 sec. It was to be just over sixteen years before the next official record for this event appeared in the I.A.A.F. list.

I saw this race in Amsterdam. A number of the runners showed considerable distress at the finish, for some had never run the distance before. There was an outcry in the Press about the folly of women running so far, with the result that the I.A.A.F. excluded the race from the Games and thirty-two years passed before it was reintroduced.

An 880 yards event was included in the Empire Games programme in 1934, but the race was omitted from the next Empire Games in 1938, and not reintroduced until 1962. The event was not included in the European Championships until 1954, the first major meeting to recognise the sense of such a race.

Between 1928 and 1953, the world record was reduced to 2 min. 7·3 sec., the two outstanding performers being Anna Larsson, of Sweden, and Nina Otkalenko of U.S.S.R. The Russian girl was the first to beat 2 min. 10·0 sec. in 1952, and the following year recorded 2 min. 7·3 sec.

Nina won the European title in 2 min. 8·6 sec., ahead of Britain's Diane Leather, who a couple of months earlier had set up a world 880 yards record of 2 min. 9·0 sec. In September 1955, Nina placed her name for the fifth and last time on the world record list with 2 min. 5·0 sec.

She did not defend her title at the Stockholm European Championships in 1958, the winner being another Russian, Yelizaveta Yermolayeva, in 2 min. 6·3 sec., with Diane Leather again taking the silver medal, three-tenths of a second behind, in her best time ever and a new United Kingdom national record.

In July 1960, the Russian girl Lyudmila Shevtsova set up a new world record of 2 min. 4·3 sec., and in March 1962, Dixie Willis, of Australia, was timed at 2 min. 1·2 sec., for a world 800 metres record during an 880-yard world record run.

It was not until 1971 that a woman officially ran the distance inside two minutes, when Hildegarde Falck of Germany, returned 1 min. 58·5 sec.

In 1964, three days after losing the Olympic 400 metres to Betty Cuthbert and having run 800 metres on only seven occasions before the Olympic final, Britain's Ann Packer ran a superb race to win by four-fifths of a second from Maryvonne Dupureur of France, in the new world record time of 2 min. 1·1 sec.

Then, in London four years later, Yugoslavian Vera Nikolic set up a world record of 2 min. 0·5 sec., just three months before the Mexico Olympics.

In Mexico, however, after winning her heat convincingly, Miss Nikolic failed to finish in the semi-final. The gold medallist was American Madeline Manning in a new Olympic time of 2 min. 0·9 sec. Miss Nikolic finished third to Lillian Board in the 1968 European event, and two years later, in Helsinki, again won the European title in 2 min. exactly. Pat Lowe and Rosemary Stirling of Great Britain finished in second and third positions, both running their best-ever races.

Some idea of the ever-increasing improvement in the standard of women's 800-metre running may be gauged from the fact that in 1960, thirteen athletes beat 2 min. 7·0 sec., yet in 1970 that number was sixty-eight.

America's Madeline Manning (No. 97), who finished more than ten yards ahead of Ileana Silai of Rumania in the 1968 Olympic 800 metres final, in 2 min. 0·9 sec.

Rosemary Stirling of Scotland just beats Pat Lowe (Eng) and Cheryl Peasley (Aus) in the 800 metres Commonwealth championship. A yard covered the first three

800 METRES · OLYMPIC CHAMPIONS

1928	Lina Radke (Germany)	
1932–56	Not held	
1960	Lyudmila Shevtsova (USSR)	
1964	Ann Packer (GB)	
1968	Madeline Manning (USA)	

POST WORLD WAR II

2:15 2:10 2:05 2:00 1:55

1,500 Metres

This event, scheduled for the first time in the Olympic Games at Munich, 1972, was included in the European Championships in 1969 and again in 1971. It was also run in the Commonwealth Games in 1970. The distance was not recognised as a world record until 1967, when Anne Smith, of Great Britain, returned 4 min. 17·3 sec. In the 1969 European Championships in Athens, Jaroslav Jehlickova, of Jugoslavia, won in the new world record time of 4 min. 10·7 sec. Second was Mia Gommers of the Netherlands in 4 min. 11·9 sec., and third was Paolo Pigni of Italy in 4 min. 12·0 sec. All three beat Paolo's world record of 4 min. 12·4 sec. which she had made two months previously.

Mia Gommers had already lowered Miss Smith's initial world record with 4 min. 15·6 sec. in October 1967. Rita Ridley finished seventh in 4 min. 15·9 sec., which was a new U.K. record — and in 1970 she reduced this to 4 min. 15·4 sec. when winning the Commonwealth title. The following year, in the Women's A.A.A. 1971 Championships, Miss Ridley set up a new U.K. record of 4 min. 14·3 sec.

At the European Championships in Helsinki in August of the same year, Karin Burneleit, of East Germany, won in the new world record time of 4 min. 9·6 sec. and Rita Ridley again bettered her own U.K. record with 4 min. 12·7 sec.

Russia held championships for women over 1,500 metres before the second world war. In 1938, Yevdokiya Vasilyeva did 4 min. 48·8 sec., and twelve years later she became world record-holder for the 800 metres. England held championships over one mile in 1936, but most other countries only introduced the 1,500 metres in the 1960s.

Right: Rita Ridley, United Kingdom record-holder for 1,500 metres (4 min. 12·7 sec.). She won the first Commonwealth 1,500 metres title in 1970 in 4 min. 18·8 sec.

Above: Karen Burneleit (GDR) setting up a new world record of 4 min. 9·6 sec. in the 1971 European 1,500 metres title

Above: Anne Smith (GB), first holder of the women's world records for 1,500 metres (4 min. 17·3 sec.) and one mile (4 min. 37·0 sec.)

80/100 Metres Hurdles

From 1932 to 1968, this event was over 80 metres, which is 87½ yards. The hurdles were 2 ft. 6 in. high, and there were eight flights spaced eight and three-quarter yards apart.

The new event over 100 metres, introduced into the 1972 Munich Games, consists of ten hurdles each 2 ft. 9 in. high and eleven yards apart. The new distance was included in the European Championships in 1969, when it was won by Karin Balzer of East Germany, in 13·3 sec. In June of 1969, Karin, who had won the Olympic 80 metres hurdles gold medal in 1964 and finished fifth in Mexico in 1968, shared the initial world record with the Polish athlete Teresa Sukniewicz with a time of 13·3 sec. She lowered it to 13·0 sec. in July and to 12·9 sec. in September.

In 1970, both these athletes again lowered the record to 12·7 sec., and in 1971, Karin retained her European title in 12·9 sec. The same year, at the age of thirty-three, she reduced the record to 12·6 sec.

In the Commonwealth Games in 1970, the winner was Pamela Kilborn of Australia. With 13·2 sec., she was well ahead of Maureen Caird, another Australian who had also won the gold medal for the 80 metres event in Mexico. This was Pamela's third victory in the Commonwealth hurdles, which she won in 1962 and was to win again in 1966. She had also won gold medals in the Commonwealth long jump in 1962, and was a member of the victorious Australian relay team of 1966 and 1970. She was awarded the M.B.E. in the 1971 Birthday Honours List.

Though the 80 metres event has now been changed to 100 metres, the history of women's hurdling is interesting.

The first Olympic hurdles champion was that great all-round athlete, Mildred Didrikson. She was followed by Trebisonda Valla of Italy, and Fanny Blankers-Koen from the Netherlands, both of whom were world record-holders.

Fanny was the first woman to record "even" time of 11 sec. This was equalled by Shirley de la Hunty of Australia, in the preliminary round of the 1952 Olympic Games, and reduced to 10·9 sec. in the final. Shirley retained her gold medal in 1956 in 10·7 sec. The German, Kreszentia Gastl, who had set up a world record of 10·6 sec. earlier in the year, did not reach the final.

Irina Press of the U.S.S.R., and one of the famous Press sisters, won in Rome ahead of Britain's Carole Quinton, but was fourth in 1964. Then in 1965, Irina reduced the world record to 10·3 sec. The final entry in the world record list for the 80 metres hurdles is 10·2 sec. — to the credit of Vera Korsakova, of U.S.S.R. who did not reach the final in Mexico.

Top: Karin Balzer (GDR), winner of the Olympic 80 metres hurdles in 1964, the European 80 metres hurdles in 1966, the 100 metres hurdles in 1969 and 1971, and world record-holder for that event

Centre: Olympic 80 metres hurdles winner in 1968, Maureen Caird has been chosen to represent Australia in the 100 metres, 100 metres hurdles and relay in Munich

Above: Irina Press (USSR), holder of world records for the 80 metres hurdles and pentathlon, Olympic hurdles champion in 1960 and pentathlon gold medallist in 1964

Above: Pam Kilborn (Aus), Commonwealth gold medallist for the hurdles on three occasions and holder of Commonwealth records for 100 and 200 metres hurdles

Relays

The sprint relay was one of the five women's events included in the 1928 Olympic Games, when the Canadian team won in 48·4 sec. It was not until 1936 that the I.A.A.F. took over the recognition of women's world records, so the time of 46·4 sec., achieved by the German team in the heats of the Berlin Olympics was the first recognised record.

Of the nineteen world records for this event in the I.A.A.F. book, thirteen were made in the Olympic Games. The U.S.A. claim six, the U.S.S.R. five, Germany four, Australia three and the Netherlands one. It is interesting to reflect that the time for the women's sprint relay bears fairly close comparison with the world record for the men's individual 400 metres.

The 1936 Olympic final produced a mild sensation. In the heats, the German team set up a new world record of 46·4 sec. But in the final, when leading by several yards, they dropped the baton during the final change over, and the U.S.A. team went on to win by seven-tenths of a second from Great Britain in 46·9 sec.

In 1952, Australia won their heat in the new Olympic and world record of 46·1 sec., but in the final their baton was dropped as it was passed from Winsome Cripps to Marjorie Jackson. Although the baton bounced and was caught by Miss Jackson, the time lost could not be regained and Australia finished fifth in 46·5 sec. The United States just beat Germany in 45·9 sec., both being credited with a new world record.

Between 1952 and the opening of the 1956 Olympics in Melbourne in December, Russian and German teams reduced the world record to 45·1 sec.

In the final of the Melbourne Olympics, Germany, through poor baton-changing, finished last in 47·2 sec. Great Britain led until the final change, and over the last fifty metres a fine struggle took place between Betty Cuthbert and Heather Armitage. Betty Cuthbert took the Australian team to victory in the new world record time of 44·5 sec.

Four years later, the first negress to win an Olympic gold medal for sprinting, American Wilma Rudolph, emulated Betty Cuthbert by her hat-trick in winning the 100 and 200 metres as well as anchoring a successful sprint relay team.

Though the U.S.A. subsequently beat the world record with a 43·9 sec. in the Tokyo Olympics, it was Poland who gained the gold with 43·6 sec. The Polish anchor runner, Ewa Klobukowska, was disqualified and the world record removed from the books, though the Olympic victory still stands. The high altitude in Mexico was favourable to sprinters and the U.S.A. improved their time to 42·8 sec.

In the 1969 European Championships, East Germany won in 43·6 sec., and two years later West Germany set up a new European record of 43·3 sec.

The 4×400 metres relay becomes a new Olympic event at the Munich Games. It was included for the first time in the European Championships in Athens, in 1969, and produced a magnificent final.

In June of 1969, a Great Britain team which included Lillian Board, the silver medallist in the 400 metres in Mexico, and Janet Simpson who was fourth in Mexico, had set up a world record of 3 min. 37·6 sec., and just over a fortnight later a French team had run in 3 min. 33·9 sec.

In the heats of the relay in Athens, West Germany took three-tenths of a second off the French time.

In the last stage of the European final, Lillian Board ran the finest race of her brilliant career, enabling Great Britain to win the gold, and share the world record time of 3 min. 30·8 sec. with the French.

East Germany won the European final in Helsinki, 1971 by nearly four seconds to set another new world record time of 3 min. 29·3 sec. That team included Helga Seidler, winner of the individual 400 metres, and Ingelore Lohse, who was third in that event.

Top left: The dropped baton which cost the Australian women's team victory in 1952

Above left: German Democratic Republic (2nd), Germany (1st) and the Soviet Union (3rd) on the victory stand at Helsinki. Germany set up a new European record of 43·3 sec.

Top right: Outside Buckingham Palace: the British women's teams after receiving world record plaques from H.R.H. Prince Philip for records in the 4×110 yards and 4×200 metres relays
Above right: Wyomia Tyus takes over the baton for the anchor stage and the United States gain a "gold" and a world record at Mexico

RELAYS · OLYMPIC CHAMPIONS

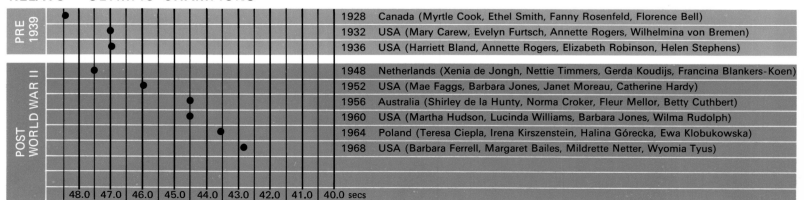

PRE 1939	1928	Canada (Myrtle Cook, Ethel Smith, Fanny Rosenfeld, Florence Bell)	
	1932	USA (Mary Carew, Evelyn Furtsch, Annette Rogers, Wilhelmina von Bremen)	
	1936	USA (Harriett Bland, Annette Rogers, Elizabeth Robinson, Helen Stephens)	
POST WORLD WAR II	1948	Netherlands (Xenia de Jongh, Nettie Timmers, Gerda Koudijs, Francina Blankers-Koen)	
	1952	USA (Mae Faggs, Barbara Jones, Janet Moreau, Catherine Hardy)	
	1956	Australia (Shirley de la Hunty, Norma Croker, Fleur Mellor, Betty Cuthbert)	
	1960	USA (Martha Hudson, Lucinda Williams, Barbara Jones, Wilma Rudolph)	
	1964	Poland (Teresa Ciepla, Irena Kirszenstein, Halina Górecka, Ewa Klobukowska)	
	1968	USA (Barbara Ferrell, Margaret Bailes, Mildrette Netter, Wyomia Tyus)	

48.0 47.0 46.0 45.0 44.0 43.0 42.0 41.0 40.0 secs

Women's Field Events

Tamara Press (USSR), holder of six world records for the shot and six for the discus; Olympic shot champion in 1960 and 1964, and discus champion in 1964; European shot champion in 1962, and discus champion in 1958 and 1962. She put the shot 61 ft. and the discus 195 ft. 10 in.

The women's Olympic field events programme originally included only the high jump and discus. It now comprises those two events together with the long jump, shot, javelin and pentathlon. I give the world records for these events in 1936 and 1971 showing also the percentage increase in performance:

	1936		1971		percentage improvement
	ft.	in.	ft.	in.	
High jump	5	5	6	3½	16%
Long jump	19	7½	22	5¼	14
Shot	47	2¼	67	0½	42
Discus	158	6	212	10	34
Javelin	153	4	204	8	33
Pentathlon	4,391 points		5,406 points		19

The specially dramatic improvement in the ''heavy'' events must very largely be due to specialisation and, of course, many more athletes in action. Here are some of the outstanding Olympic performances which I recall.

1932 Los Angeles
Mildred Didrikson won the javelin and was second in the high jump, sharing the world record with Jean Shiley, but not the ''gold'', which went to Jean.

1936 Berlin
A long-drawn-out duel in the high jump with sixteen-year-old Dorothy Odam losing the ''gold'' in the jump-off. Had the new rule, passed after the Games, for deciding ''ties'' been in operation, Dorothy would have been the champion.

1948 London
Another fine duel in the high jump, the last event of the Games which thousands stayed to watch. Though Dorothy Tyler cleared the same height as the winner, Alice Coachman, she again lost the ''gold'' under the ''tie-break'' rules.

1952 Helsinki
The first appearance of the Russians, who gained seven places out of nine in the shot, discus and javelin. Yvette Williams, who won the long jump for New Zealand with a leap within one centimetre of the world record, was awarded the MBE.

1956 Melbourne
American Mildred McDaniel won the high jump easily with over 5 ft. 9 in. Olga Connolly of Czechoslovakia prevented a Russian ''hat-trick'' in the throwing events by winning the discus.

1960 Rome
The first victory of Iolanda Balas in the high jump. The Roumanian, who had already achieved nine world records and was next year to add four more to this total, cleared over 6 feet.

1964 Tokyo
A repeat victory for Balas with 6 ft. 2¾ in., and a great victory for Mary Rand in the long jump, with a new world record — the first Olympic ''gold'' for Britain in women's athletics and the first woman over 22 feet.

1968 Mexico
A breach in Russian supremacy. Margitta Gummel of East Germany won the shot with a new world record. A world record in the long jump by the Roumanian Viorica Viscopoleanu, while her compatriot Lia Manoliu won the discus with a new Olympic record.

Mary Rand, Britain's first-ever women's Olympic champion, at practice

High Jump

It is perhaps possible to emphasise the truly remarkable progress in women's high jumping since the second world war, by mentioning that the present world record of 6 ft. 3½ in. would have won the men's Olympic gold medal in 1908, and the bronze medal in 1928. This is the outstanding athletic event in which women have most nearly approached the standard of men.

It was in October 1958, that Iolanda Balas of Roumania became the first woman to clear six feet, eighty-six years after man had "unbelievably" soared to such heights. Miss Balas will always rank as a phenomenal performer. During her career, which lasted from 1951 when she won the first of sixteen Roumanian titles with a leap of 4 ft. 10¼ in., to 1966, she cleared six feet on fifty occasions. Over a period of five years almost to the day, she broke the world record fourteen times. Her final jump of 6 ft. 3¼ in. remained a record for ten years, until 1971 when Ilona Gusenbauer of Austria, mother of a two-year-old baby and 1971 European champion, cleared 6 ft. 3½ in. This leap was five inches above her own head.

Six feet is now almost commonplace for a woman, no less than eleven athletes having cleared that height in 1971.

Great Britain's women athletes did not take part in the 1928 Games, and had no competitor in the high jump at Los Angeles in 1932. But in Berlin in 1936, Dorothy Odam, a sixteen-and-a-half-year-old schoolgirl, gained a silver medal. In fact, she cleared the same height, 5 ft. 3 in., as the winner, Ibolya Csak of Hungary. However, under the rules then operating in the "jump-off", the Hungarian gained the gold.

A few days later, the present rules were accepted by the authorities. These state that it must be considered whether the athletes tieing, cleared the tieing height with the same number of jumps and, if not, the athlete with the fewer number is awarded the title. Had the new rule been in existence in Berlin, Dorothy would have been Great Britain's first Olympic track and field gold medallist. Twelve years later, Dorothy, now married with two children and competing as Mrs. Tyler, again tied with the gold medallist, Alice Coachman. Both cleared 5 ft. 6⅛ in. for a new Olympic record, but Dorothy took more jumps to do it and again had to be content with the silver.

In the Rome Olympics, when Miss Balas raised the Olympic record to 6 ft. 0¾ in., Dorothy Shirley tied for second place with 5 ft. 7¼ in.

This was the last time Great Britain was placed in the Olympic high jump, but in the 1962 European Championships, sixteen-year-old Linda Knowles gained the bronze. Then,

in 1971, Barbara Inkpen employed the "Fosbury Flop", and tied for Europe's second place. In 1971, both Linda and Barbara cleared six feet. Without question, British women athletes have done better in the high jump than any other event.

Above left: Canada's Debbie Brill, Commonwealth champion in 1970 at the age of seventeen, using the "Brill bend", a feminine version of the "Fosbury flop".

Above right: Changing from a "straddle" jumper to a "Fosbury flopper" just before the European Championships, Barbara Inkpen (GB) improved her high jump by two inches to set up a new United Kingdom record of 6 ft. 0¾ in.

HIGH JUMP · OLYMPIC CHAMPIONS

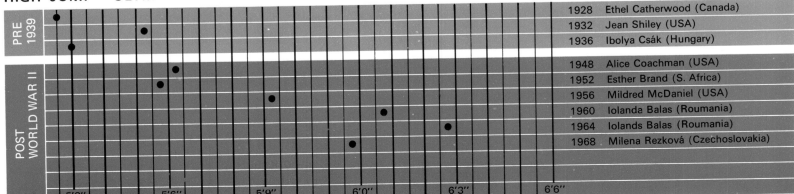

PRE 1939	1928	Ethel Catherwood (Canada)
	1932	Jean Shiley (USA)
	1936	Ibolya Csák (Hungary)
POST WORLD WAR II	1948	Alice Coachman (USA)
	1952	Esther Brand (S. Africa)
	1956	Mildred McDaniel (USA)
	1960	Iolanda Balas (Roumania)
	1964	Iolanda Balas (Roumania)
	1968	Milena Rezková (Czechoslovakia)

Long Jump

The women's long jump was not included in the Olympic Games until 1948, despite the fact that it had featured in all women's athletic programmes since the real commencement of women's athletics in the early 1920s.

Although 20 ft. had first been reached by a woman in 1939, and the superb Fanny Blankers-Koen had raised the record to 20 ft. 6 in. during the war, she did not compete in that event in the 1948 Olympics, which was won with the distance of 18 ft. 8¼ in. Four years later, Yvette Williams of New Zealand won with just four inches to spare with 20 ft. 5¾ in., one centimetre less than the world record, which Yvette herself improved to 20 ft. 7½ in. some eighteen months later.

In August 1956 Elzbieta Krzesinska of Poland took the record to within two inches of 21 ft., and in winning the Olympic "gold" in Melbourne, with over ten inches to spare, the Polish girl equalled her own world record. In August 1960, Hildrun Klaus of Germany became the first woman to clear 21 ft., but Klaus finished "only third" in the Rome Olympics with 20 ft. 4½ in., six inches behind Vyera Krepkina of the U.S.S.R., who beat the holder by four inches.

In the qualifying round for the Tokyo Olympics, Mary Rand led the field with her best ever jump of 21 ft. 7½ in., and a new Olympic record. In the competition proper she improved to 21 ft. 9 in., and finally to a new world record of 22 ft. 2¼ in., to win by six-and-a-half inches from the Polish jumper Irena Kirszenstein, with the Russian Tatyana Shchelkanova third, another seven inches away.

The world record remained intact until the Mexico Olympics when, with her first jump, Viorica Viscopoleanu of Roumania beat Mary Rand's record with a leap of 22 ft. 4½ in. In 1970, Heide Rosendahl of Germany raised the world record to 22 ft. 5¼ in.

In Mexico, ten athletes beat 21 ft. In 1971 the world ranking list shows three competitors over 22 ft., and no less than twenty-five over 21 ft. Will someone approach 23 ft. in Munich? And can Sheila Sherwood, who in the 1970 Commonwealth Games won the title with 22 ft. 1 in., and had five other jumps within two inches of this, retain her silver medal, or even move into the "gold" standard?

Top left: In Mexico Sheila Sherwood (GB) gained a silver medal in the long jump, while her husband John won a bronze in the 400 metres hurdles. Both gained "golds" at the 1970 Commonwealth Games. Sheila's long jump was a United Kingdom All-comers' record

Above left: 1st, Ingrid Becker (Ger), 2nd, Meta Artenen (Swi) and 3rd, Heide Rosendahl (Ger). With a leap of 22 ft. 2¼ in. Becker beat the Swiss girl by one and a quarter inches

Top right: In 1971 Heide Rosendhal raised the world record by three-quarters of an inch to 22 ft. 5¼ in.

Above right: With a new world record of 22 ft. 4½ in., Viorica Viscopoleanu (Rou) claimed the "gold" in Mexico. Her jump was two inches further than Mary Rand's record win four years before to the day

LONG JUMP · OLYMPIC CHAMPIONS

POST WORLD WAR II						
1928–36	Not held					
1948	Olga Gyarmati (Hungary)					
1952	Yvette Williams (New Zealand)					
1956	Elzbieta Krzesinska (Poland)					
1960	Vyera Krepkina (USSR)					
1964	Mary Rand (GB)					
1968	Viorica Viscopoleanu (Rou)					

19'0''   20'0''   21'0''   22'0''   23'0''   24'0''

Putting the Shot

Putting the shot — the women's shot weighs 4 kilos — was another event not introduced into the Olympics until after the second world war. In the 1920s, the event was decided by aggregate performances with both hands. It was not until 1930 that in the women's British event, the single-handed test was introduced. In 1934 at the first Empire Games a shot contest was included.

The first world record in the "official" list, so far as the 4 kilos shot is concerned, stands to the credit of Gisela Mauermayer of Germany. In 1934 she reached 47 ft. 2¼ in. — a record which stood for fourteen years.

At the Olympic Games in 1952, the Russian Galina Zybina became the first woman to beat 50 ft., winning by over two feet. She dominated the shot-putting world for many years, securing no less than eight world record plaques, raising the world record to 55 ft., and taking part in four Olympics. As late as 1964 at the Tokyo Olympics, and at the age of thirty-three, she did her best-ever putt of 57 ft. 3 in. to gain the bronze medal.

In 1960, Tamara Press (U.S.S.R.) became the first woman to beat 58 ft., and five years later reached 61 ft. In April 1968 yet another Russian, Nadyezhda Chizhova putt 61 ft. 3 in., but in September Margitta Gummel of East Germany got within one inch of 62 ft. In winning the gold medal in Mexico, the German first raised the world best to 62 ft. 6¾ in., and then to 64 ft. 4 in. Chizhova had to be content with the bronze medal with 59 ft. 8¼ in.

In May 1969, Chizhova regained the world record with 64 ft. 8½ in., and in July was within an inch of 66 ft. Less than a week before the 1969 European Championships, Gummel made her fourth appearance in the world record role, with just half an inch short of 66 ft. The two occupied first and second places in the Championships in Athens in September. Chizhova equalled Gummel's world record with her first putt, and with her final putt reached 67 ft. 0½ in. — a distance she repeated in 1971.

Top: A month after setting up a new world record of 61 ft. 11 in., Margitta Gummel (GDR) first reached 62 ft. 6¾ in. and then 64 ft. 4 in. to win the Olympic "gold" in Mexico

Above: Though some eighteen inches below her United Kingdom record of 1966, Mary Peters won the Commonwealth title in 1970. Here she is competing in Tokyo.

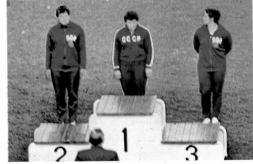

Nadyezhda Chizhova (USSR), three times European champion and present world record-holder with 67 ft. 0½ in. She has held the world record six times

PUTTING THE SHOT · OLYMPIC CHAMPIONS

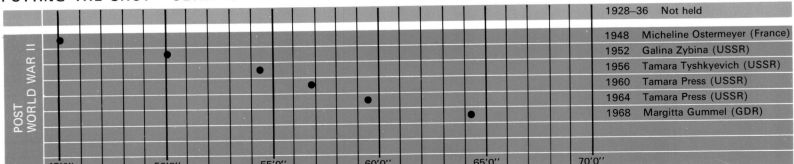

1928–36	Not held	
1948	Micheline Ostermeyer (France)	
1952	Galina Zybina (USSR)	
1956	Tamara Tyshkyevich (USSR)	
1960	Tamara Press (USSR)	
1964	Tamara Press (USSR)	
1968	Margitta Gummel (GDR)	

POST WORLD WAR II

45'0''   50'0''   55'0''   60'0''   65'0''   70'0''

Throwing the Discus

The women's discus weighs 1 kilo — just half the weight of the men's discus. It was the only "strong women's" event introduced into the 1928 Olympic Games. It was won with just under 130 ft. Prior to the 1936 Games, Gisela Mauermayer of Germany set up a world record of 158 ft. 6 in.

Mauermayer's record stood for over twelve years, when the first of the great Russian performers, Nina Dumbadze, added over sixteen feet to the distance. Dumbadze was third in the 1952 Olympics, in which the Russian women, entering the Olympics for the first time, secured all three medals. The winner was Nina Romashkova, perhaps better known as Ponomaryeva, who threw 168 ft. 8½ in. — good enough to give her victory by over fourteen feet. Three weeks later she added ten inches to Dumbadze's world record, but within two months Dumbadze threw 187 ft. 2 in. — a record which was to stand for eight years.

In the Rome Olympics Dumbadze won the title again with over 180 ft., though exactly a week later Tamara Press was to achieve the first of her six world records with 187 ft. 7 in. In 1963 Press raised the world record to 194 ft. 6 in., and in 1965 added yet another sixteen inches to the record.

In 1967 Liesel Westermann of West Germany became the first woman to exceed 200 ft., with a new world record of 201 ft. exactly. The following May, Christine Spielberg of East Germany added fifteen inches to Liesel's world record, but within two months Liesel recaptured the world title with 205 ft. 2 in. The two met at the Mexico Olympics, but they were both below their best form, and with her first throw, Lia Manoliu of Roumania reached over 192 ft., for a new Olympic record.

In the year following the Games, Westermann improved the world record, first to 205 ft. 8 in., then to 209 ft. 10 in. In 1971 Faina Melnik of the U.S.S.R. became the first athlete to exceed 210 ft., first with 210 ft. 8 in. and later with 212 ft. 10 in.

Above: With her final throw to come, Faina Melnik (USSR) was still four feet behind Liesel Westermann (Ger), world record holder. Then Faina produced a new world record for the European title of 1971. Though twenty-six years old, 1971 was only her second season in international athletics

Right: Scotland's Rosemary Payne captured the Commonwealth discus title on the same afternoon that her husband Howard became the hammer gold medallist. Since 1964 Rosemary has raised the United Kingdom record by over twelve feet

THROWING THE DISCUS · OLYMPIC CHAMPIONS

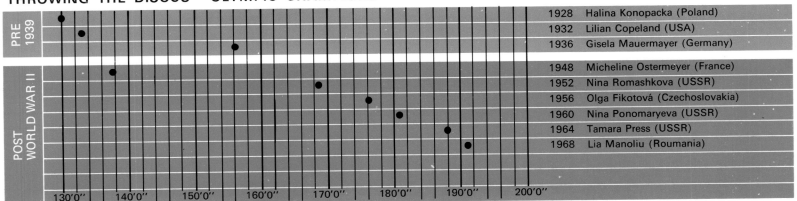

		Year	Champion
PRE 1939		1928	Halina Konopacka (Poland)
		1932	Lilian Copeland (USA)
		1936	Gisela Mauermayer (Germany)
POST WORLD WAR II		1948	Micheline Ostermeyer (France)
		1952	Nina Romashkova (USSR)
		1956	Olga Fikotová (Czechoslovakia)
		1960	Nina Ponomaryeva (USSR)
		1964	Tamara Press (USSR)
		1968	Lia Manoliu (Roumania)

130'0"   140'0"   150'0"   160'0"   170'0"   180'0"   190'0"   200'0"

Throwing the Javelin

The women's javelin weighs seven ounces less than the men's, and is over a foot shorter. Originally the women's contests were, as in the shot and discus, decided by an aggregate of both hands. The event for single-handed efforts was first introduced into the 1932 Olympics, and was included in the second Empire Games in 1934 — the first Games with any women competing — two years later.

The first winner was that great all-round athlete, Mildred Didrikson, with 143 ft. 4 in. Nan Gindele, also U.S.A., who had set up a world record of over 153 ft. two months before, was fifth with under 125 ft.

In 1949 Nataya Smirnitskaya of U.S.S.R. became the first woman to exceed first 160 and then 170 ft., but she did not compete in the 1952 Olympics, which Dana Zátopková, Czechoslovakia won the the same afternoon that her husband Emil Zatopek gained his second "gold" in the 5,000 metres.

The world record was raised to 182 ft. in 1954 by the Russian Nadyezhda Konyayeva, who gained a bronze medal in Melbourne with a throw over eighteen feet below her world record, but some eighteen inches further than Dana, who two years later, for about seven weeks, held the world record with 182 ft. 10 in. It was Anna Pazera from Poland, representing her adopted country of Australia in the Commonwealth Games, who displaced Dana's world best with 188 ft. 4 in.

In 1960 Elvira Ozolina of U.S.S.R. became the first woman to beat 190 ft. In the qualifying round in the Tokyo Olympics Yelena Gorchakova threw 204 ft. 8 in. — the present world record — but she threw over seventeen feet less in the final, which gained her the bronze. The winner was Mihaela Penes of Roumania by over seven feet, with 198 ft. $7\frac{1}{2}$ in. Elvira, who earlier in the year had become the first woman to beat 200 ft., was fifth, short of 180 ft.

Great Britain's best performer to date has been Susan Platt with 182 ft. 5 in. in 1968. She was extremely unlucky in Rome to have a throw, which many thought valid and would have given her a silver medal, disallowed.

Top: On the stand at Mexico: silver medallist Mihaela Penes (Rou), gold medallist Angela Nemeth (Hun), bronze medallist Eva Janko (Austria). With 198 ft., Angela beat the reigning Olympic champion by nineteen inches

Far left: Petra Rivers (Aus) won the 1970 Commonwealth title with only 170 ft. 7 in., but later reached 202 ft. 8 in., the world's best for the year

Left: Ameli Koloska (Ger), silver medallist with 194 ft. 10 in., and European champion Daniela Jaworska (Pol) with 200 ft. 1 in., on the victory stand at Helsinki, 1971

THROWING THE JAVELIN · OLYMPIC CHAMPIONS

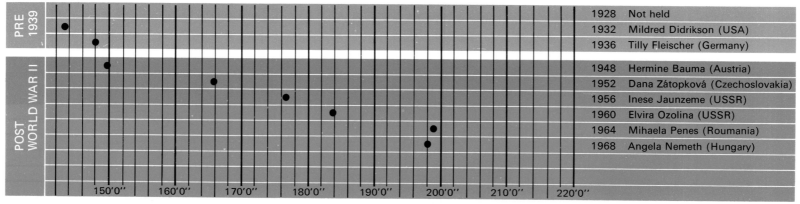

PRE 1939	1928	Not held
	1932	Mildred Didrikson (USA)
	1936	Tilly Fleischer (Germany)
POST WORLD WAR II	1948	Hermine Bauma (Austria)
	1952	Dana Zátopková (Czechoslovakia)
	1956	Inese Jaunzeme (USSR)
	1960	Elvira Ozolina (USSR)
	1964	Mihaela Penes (Roumania)
	1968	Angela Nemeth (Hungary)

150'0" 160'0" 170'0" 180'0" 190'0" 200'0" 210'0" 220'0"

The Pentathlon

The women's pentathlon consists of the following five events: 100 metres hurdles, shot putt, high jump, long jump and 200 metres. In the Olympic Games the first three events are held on the first day, the latter two on the second. Scoring is by points awarded according to a table laid down by the International Federation in 1970. This superseded a previous table made in 1954. The new table awards less points (about 15 per cent less than the old). For example, the world records for the five events under the old and new tables are as follows:

	Old (1954)	New (1970)
100 metres hurdles	1,262	1,062
High jump	1,249	1,140
Long jump	1,173	1,084
Shot putt	1,364	1,173
200 metres	1,196	1,100

The world record total number of points is 5,406 (old), 4,775 (new).

Before the second world war there was no hurdles event, a javelin constituting the fifth event. Up to 1968 the hurdles (2 ft. 6 in. high) was run over 80 metres. It is now run over 100 metres with hurdles 2 ft. 9 in. high.

A pentathlon contest was included in the 1950 European Championships, then came into the Olympics in 1964 and into the Commonwealth Games in 1970.

In the 1964 Olympics, the world record-holder Irina Press (younger sister of Tamara), had to beat her own world record to win the "gold". Her runner-up was Mary Rand, winner of the Olympic long jump. Mary actually scored more points than Irina in three of the five events, and only 35 points fewer in the hurdles. But in the shot putt, the Russian totalled no less than 384 points more than Mary, and this placed the result beyond any doubt.

In 1958 Mary set up her first United Kingdom record of 4,466 points, and her Olympic total for the silver medal of 5,035 points was another U.K. record. In 1970, Mary Peters won the Commonwealth title with a score of 5,148 for a new U.K. (national) record. Ann Wilson finished 111 points behind, also beating Mary Rand's previous U.K. record by two points, though in strict accuracy it should be mentioned that Mary's record was made with the 80 metres hurdles, the other two with a 100 metres hurdles event.

The qualifying performance for the Munich Olympics is 4,800 points calculated on the 1954 table or 4,200 points according to the new table. Last year no fewer than thirteen athletes exceeded 5,000 points under the 1954 table and another seventeen scored more than 4,800 points. The new table will be used in Munich.

Top: Heide Rosendahl (Ger) and Burglinde Pollak (GDR). In the 1971 European competition, with one event to go, world record-holder Pollak lead by six points. But Rosendahl scored thirty points more in the 200 metres, to win by 5,299 to 5,275

Centre left: Heide Rosendahl in the 100 metres hurdles, the first of the pentathlon events. After the first three events she was 136 points behind Pollak

Centre right: Ingrid Becker (Ger), gold medallist at the Mexico Olympics with 5,098 points

Right: Mary Peters of Northern Ireland, 1970 Commonwealth champion with 5,148 points, a Commonwealth record

THE PENTATHLON · OLYMPIC CHAMPIONS

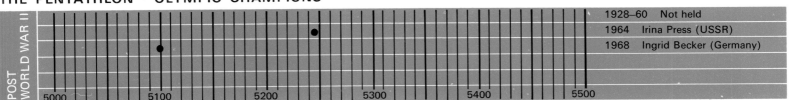

1928–60	Not held
1964	Irina Press (USSR)
1968	Ingrid Becker (Germany)

Records

World Records up to December 31st 1971

Men's Events	hr.	min.	sec.	Track
100 yards			9·1	R. Hayes (USA)
				H. Jerome (Can)
				J. Hines (USA)
				C. Greene (USA)
				J. Carlos (USA)
100 metres			9·9	C. Greene (USA)
				J. Hines (USA)
				R. R. Smith (USA)
200 metres (s)			19·5	T. Smith (USA)
200 metres (t)			19·8	T. Smith (USA)
				D. Quarrie (Jam)
220 yards (s)			19·5	T. Smith (USA)
220 yards (t)			20·0	T. Smith (USA)
400 metres			43·8	L. Evans (USA)
440 yards			44·5	J. Smith (USA)
800 metres		1	44·3	P. Snell (NZ)
				R. Doubell (Aus)
880 yards		1	44·9	J. Ryun (USA)
1,000 metres		2	16·2	J. May (GDR)
				F.-J. Kemper (Ger)
1,500 metres		3	33·1	J. Ryun (USA)
1 mile		3	51·1	J. Ryun (USA)
2,000 metres		4	56·2	M. Jazy (Fr)
3,000 metres		7	39·6	K. Keino (Ken)
2 miles		8	17·8	E. Puttemans (Bel)
3 miles		12	50·4	R. Clarke (Aus)
5,000 metres		13	16·6	R. Clarke (Aus)
6 miles		26	47·0	R. Clarke (Aus)
10,000 metres		27	39·4	R. Clarke (Aus)
10 miles		46	37·4	J. Drayton (Can)
20,000 metres		58	06·2	G. Roelants (Bel)
20,664 metres	1	00	00·0	G. Roelants (Bel)
15 miles	1	12	48·2	R. Hill (GB)
25,000 metres	1	15	22·6	R. Hill (GB)
30,000 metres	1	31	30·4	J. Alder (GB)
3,000 m. steeplechase		8	22·0	K. O'Brien (Aus)
120 yards hurdles			13·0	R. Milburn (USA)
110 m. hurdles			13·2	M. Lauer (Ger)
				L. Calhoun (USA)
				E. McCullouch (USA)
200 m. hurdles (s)			21·9	D. Styron (USA)
200 m. hurdles (t)			22·5	M. Lauer (Ger)
				G. Davis (USA)
220 yards hurdles (s)			21·9	D. Styron (USA)
400 m. hurdles			48·1	D. Hemery (GB)
440 yards hurdles			48·8	R. Mann (USA)

Relays		min.	sec.	
4×100 metres			38·2	United States
4×110 yards			38·6	United States
4×200 metres		1	21·7	United States
4×220 yards		1	21·7	United States
4×400 metres		2	56·1	United States
4×440 yards		3	02·8	Trinidad and Tobago
4×800 metres		7	08·6	Germany
4×880 yards		7	11·6	Kenya
4×1,500 metres		14	49·0	France
4×1 mile		16	09·0	United States

(s) = straight; (t) = turn.

Field	ft.	in.	metres	
High jump	7	6¼	2·29	P. Matzdorf (USA)
Pole vault	18	0	5·49	C. Papanikolaou (Gre)
Long jump	29	2½	8·90	R. Beamon (USA)
Triple jump	57	1	17·40	P. Perez (Cuba)
Shot	71	5½	21·78	R. Matson (USA)
Discus	224	5	68·40	J. Silvester (USA)
Hammer	250	8	76·40	W. Schmidt (Ger)
Javelin	304	1	92·70	J. Kinnunen (Finland)
Decathlon	8,417 points			W. Toomey (USA)

Walking	hr.	min.	sec.	
20,000 metres	1	25	50·0	P. Frenkel (GDR)
26,658 metres	2	00	00·0	P. Frenkel (GDR)
30,000 metres	2	15	16·0	C. Hohne (GDR)
20 miles	2	31	33·0	A. Vedyakov (USSR)
30 miles	3	56	12·6	P. Selzer (GDR)
50,000 metres	4	04	19·8	P. Selzer (GDR)

Women's Events	min.	sec.	Track
60 metres		7·2	B. Cuthbert (Aus)
			I. Bochkaryova (USSR)
100 yards		10·0	Chi Cheng (Tai)
100 metres		11·0	W. Tyus (USA)
			Chi Cheng (Tai)
			R. Meissner (GDR)
200 metres		22·4	Chi Cheng (Tai)
220 yards		22·6	Chi Cheng (Tai)
400 metres		51·0	M. Neufville (Jam)
440 yards		52·4	J. Amoore (Aus)
800 metres	1	58·5	H. Falck (Ger)
880 yards	2	02·0	D. Willis (Aus)
			J. Pollock (Aus)
1,500 metres	4	09·6	K. Burneleit (GDR)
1 mile	4	35·3	E. Tittel (Ger)
100 metres hurdles		12·6	K. Balzer (GDR)
200 metres hurdles		25·8	P. Kilborn (Aus)
			A. Jahns (GDR)
			T. Sukniewicz (Pol)

Relays		min.	sec.	
4×100 metres			42·8	United States
4×110 yards			44·7	United States
4×200 metres		1	33·8	Great Britain
4×220 yards		1	35·8	Australia
4×400 metres		3	29·3	GDR
4×440 yards		3	38·8	United States
4×800 metres		8	16·8	Germany

Field	ft.	in.	metres	
High jump	6	3½	1·92	I. Gusenbauer (Austria)
Long jump	22	5¼	6·84	H. Rosendahl (Ger)
Shot	67	0½	20·43	N. Chizhova (USSR)
Discus	212	10	64·88	F. Melnik (USSR)
Javelin	204	8	62·40	Y. Gorchakova (USSR)
Pentathlon	5,406 points			B. Pollak (GDR)

Key to nationality abbreviations

Australia (Aus); Austria (Aust); Belgium (Bel); Brazil (Bra); Bulgaria (Bul); Canada (Can); Czechoslovakia (Cze); England (Eng); Finland (Fin); France (Fr); Great Britain (GB); German Democratic Republic (GDR); German Federal Republic (Ger); Ghana (Gha); Greece (Gre); Holland (Neth); Hungary (Hun); Jamaica (Jam); Kenya (Ken); Korea (Kor); New Zealand (NZ); Northern Ireland (NI); Norway (Nor); Poland (Pol); Roumania (Rou); Scotland (Scot); South Africa (SA); Soviet Union (USSR); Spain (Spa); Sweden (Swe); Switzerland (Swi); Taiwan (Tai); Trinidad (Tri); Uganda (Uga); United States (USA); Yugoslavia (Yug).

European Records up to December 31st 1971

Men's Events	hr.	min.	sec.	Track
100 yards			9·4	A. Hary (Ger)
				P. Radford (GB)
100 metres			10·0	A. Hary (Ger)
				R. Bambuck (Fr)
				V. Sapeya (USSR)
				V. Borzov (USSR)
				G. Metz (Ger)
				M. Kokot (GDR)
200 metres			20·2	V. Borzov (USSR)
220 yards			20·5	P. Radford (GB)
400 metres			44·9	C. Kaufmann (Ger)
				M. Jellinghaus (Ger)
440 yards			45·9	R. Brightwell (GB)
800 metres		1	44·9	F.-J. Kemper (Ger)
				W. Adams (Ger)
880 yards		1	46·7	J. Plachy (Cze)
1,000 metres		2	16·2	J. May (GDR)
				F.-J. Kemper (Ger)
1,500 metres		3	34·0	J. Wadoux (Fr)
1 mile		3	53·6	M. Jazy (Fr)
2,000 metres		4	56·2	M. Jazy (Fr)
3,000 metres		7	39·8	E. Puttemans (Bel)
2 miles		8	17·8	E. Puttemans (Bel)
3 miles		12	58·2	D. Bedford (GB)
5,000 metres		13	22·2	D. Bedford (GB)
6 miles		26	51·6	D. Bedford (GB)
10,000 metres		27	47·0	D. Bedford (GB)
10 miles		46	44·0	R. Hill (GB)
20,000 metres		58	06·2	G. Roelants (Bel)
20,664 metres	1	00	00·0	G. Roelants (Bel)
15 miles	1	12	48·2	R. Hill (GB)
25,000 metres	1	15	22·6	R. Hill (GB)
30,000 metres	1	31	30·4	J. Alder (GB)
3,000 m. steeplechase		8	22·2	V. Dudin (USSR)
110 m. hurdles			13·2	M. Lauer (Ger)
200 m. hurdles			22·5	M. Lauer (Ger)
400 m. hurdles			48·1	D. Hemery (GB)
440 yd. hurdles			50·1	S. Morale (Italy)

Relays		min.	sec.	
4×100 metres			38·4	France
4×110 yards			40·0	Great Britain
4×200 metres		1	22·4	Germany
4×400 metres		3	00·5	Poland: Germany
4×440 yards		3	06·5	Great Britain
4×800 metres		7	08·6	Germany
4×880 yards		7	14·6	Germany
4×1,500 metres		14	49·0	France
4×1 mile		16	09·6	Germany

Field	ft.	in.	metres	
High jump	7	5¾	2·28	V. Brumel (USSR)
Pole vault	18	0	5·49	C. Papanikolaou (Gre)
Long jump	27	4¾	8·35	I. Ter-Ovanesian (USSR)
				J. Schwarz (Ger)
Triple jump	57	0¾	17·39	V. Saneyev (USSR)
Shot	69	3½	21·12	H.-J. Rothenburg (GDR)
Discus	223	3	68·06	R. Bruch (Swe)
Hammer	250	8	76·40	W. Schmidt (Ger)
Javelin	304	1	92·70	J. Kinnunen (Fin)
Decathlon	8,319 points			K. Bendlin (Ger)

Walking	hr.	min.	sec.	
20,000 metres	1	25	50·0	P. Frenkel (GDR)
26,658 metres	2	00	00·0	P. Frenkel (GDR)
30,000 metres	2	15	16·0	C. Höhne (GDR)
20 miles	2	31	33·0	A. Vedyakov (USSR)
30 miles	3	56	12·6	P. Selzer (GDR)
50,000 metres	4	04	19·8	P. Selzer (GDR)

Women's Events		min.	sec.	Track
100 yards			10·5	I. Kirszenstein (Pol)
100 metres			11·0	R. Meissner (GDR)
200 metres			22·5	I. Szewinska (Pol)
220 yards			23·6	M. Itkina (USSR)
				D. Arden (GB)
				I. Szewinska (Pol)
400 metres			51·7	N. Duclos (Fr)
				C. Besson (Fr)
440 yards			53·7	M. Itkina (USSR)
800 metres		1	58·5	H. Falck (Ger)
880 yards		2	03·0	V. Nikolic (Yug)
1,500 metres		4	09·6	K. Burneleit (GDR)
1 mile		4	35·3	E. Tittel (Ger)
100 m. hurdles			12·6	K. Balzer (GDR)
200 m. hurdles			25·8	A. Jahns (GDR)
				T. Sukniewicz (Pol)

Relays		min.	sec.	
4×100 metres			43·3	Germany
4×110 yards			45·0	Great Britain
4×200 metres		1	33·8	Great Britain
4×220 yards		1	36·0	GDR
4×400 metres		3	29·3	GDR
4×800 metres		8	16·8	Germany

Field	ft.	in.	metres	
High jump	6	3½	1·92	I. Gusenbauer (Austria)
Long jump	22	5¼	6·84	H. Rosendahl (Ger)
Shot	67	0½	20·43	N. Chizhova (USSR)
Discus	212	10	64·88	F. Melnik (USSR)
Javelin	204	8	62·40	Y. Gorchakova (USSR)
Pentathlon	5,406 points			B. Pollak (GDR)

Commonwealth Records up to December 31st 1971

Men's Events

Men's Events	hr.	min.	sec.	Track
100 yards			9·1	H. Jerome (Can)
100 metres			10·0	H. Jerome (Can)
				L. Miller (Jam)
200 metres			19·8	D. Quarrie (Jam)
220 yards (s)			20·1	M. Agostini (Trin)
				E. Roberts (Trin)
200 yards (t)			20·4	H. Jerome (Can)
				L. Miller (Jam)
400 metres			45·0	W. Mottley (Trin)
				C. Asati (Ken)
440 yards			45·0	W. Mottley (Trin)
800 metres		1	44·3	R. Doubell (Aus)
				P. Snell (NZ)
880 yards		1	45·1	P. Snell (NZ)
1,000 metres		2	16·6	P. Snell (NZ)
1,500 metres		3	34·9	K. Keino (Ken)
1 mile		3	53·1	K. Keino (Ken)
2,000 metres		5	05·2	K. Keino (Ken)
3,000 metres		7	39·6	K. Keino (Ken)
2 miles		8	19·6	R. Clarke (Aus)
3 miles		12	50·4	R. Clarke (Aus)
5,000 metres		13	16·6	R. Clarke (Aus)
6 miles		26	47·0	R. Clarke (Aus)
10,000 metres		27	39·4	R. Clarke (Aus)
10 miles		46	37·4	J. Drayton (Can)
20,000 metres		58	39·0	R. Hill (Eng)
20,471 metres	1	00	00·0	R. Hill (Eng)
15 miles	1	12	48·2	R. Hill (Eng)
25,000 metres	1	15	22·6	R. Hill (Eng)
30,000 metres	1	31	30·4	J. Alder (Scot)
3,000 m. steeplechase		8	22·0	K. O'Brien (Aus)
110 m. hurdles			13·6	D. Hemery (Eng)
200 m. hurdles			22·7	J. McCann (Aus)
400 m. hurdles			48·1	D. Hemery (Eng)
440 yd. hurdles			49·3	G. Potgieter (SA)

Relays

Relays		min.	sec.	
4×100 metres			38·3	Jamaica
4×110 yards			39·8	Ghana
4×200 metres		1	23·5	Trinidad and Tobago
4×220 yards		1	23·9	Southern Transvaal
4×400 metres		2	59·6	Kenya
4×440 yards		3	02·8	Trinidad and Tobago
4×800 metres		7	11·6	Kenya
4×880 yards		7	11·6	Kenya
4×1,500 metres		15	06·6	Great Britain
4×1 mile		16	23·8	New Zealand

Field

Field	ft.	in.	metres	
High jump	7	3	2·21	P. Boyce (Aus)
Pole vault	17	4	5·28	K. Bryde (Can)
Long jump	27	0	8·23	L. Davies (Wales)
Shot	64	11¾	19·80	L. Mills (NZ)
Discus	211	3	64·40	G. Puce (Can)
Hammer	227	2	69·24	H. Payne (Eng)
Javelin	273	9	83·44	D. Travis (Eng)
Decathlon	7,903 points			P. Gabbett (Eng)

Walking

Walking	hr.	min.	sec.	
2 miles		13	02·4	S. Vickers (Eng)
5 miles		34	21·2	K. Matthews (Eng)
10,000 metres		41	55·6	P. Embleton (Eng)
7 miles		48	22·2	K. Matthews (Eng)
20,000 metres	1	28	45·8	K. Matthews (Eng)
26,117 metres	2	00	00·0	E. Allsopp (Aus)
30,000 metres	2	25	02·2	N. Freeman (Aus)
20 miles	2	37	51·8	N. Freeman (Aus)
30 miles	4	08	11·6	D. Thompson (Eng)
50,000 metres	4	17	29·8	D. Thompson (Eng)

Women's Events

Women's Events	min.	sec.	Track
100 yards		10·3	M. Willard (Aus)
100 metres		11·1	R. Boyle (Aus)
200 metres		22·7	R. Boyle (Aus)
220 yards		22·9	M. Burvill (Aus)
400 metres		51·0	M. Neufville (Jam)
440 yards		52·4	J. Pollock (Aus)
800 metres	2	01·0	J. Pollock (Aus)
880 yards	2	02·0	D. Willis (Aus)
			J. Pollock (Aus)
1,500 metres	4	12·7	R. Ridley (Eng)
1 mile	4	37·0	A. Smith (Eng)
100 m. hurdles		13·1	P. Kilborn (Aus)
200 m. hurdles		25·8	P. Kilborn (Aus)

Relays

Relays		min.	sec.	Track
4×100 metres			43·4	Australia
4×110 yards			45·0	Great Britain
4×200 metres		1	33·8	Great Britain
4×220 yards		1	35·8	Australia
4×400 metres		3	30·8	Great Britain
4×800 metres		8	23·8	Great Britain

Field

Field	ft.	in.	metres	
High jump	6	0¾	1·85	B. Inkpen (Eng)
				D. Brill (Can)
Long jump	22	2¼	6·76	M. Rand (Eng)
Shot	56	7½	17·26	V. Young (NZ)
Discus	180	7	55·04	R. Payne (Scot)
Javelin	202	8	61·78	P. Rivers (Aus)
Pentathlon	5,148 points			M. Peters (NI)

United Kingdom (National) Records up to December 31st 1971

Men's Events	hr.	min.	sec.	Track
100 yards			9·4	P. Radford
100 metres			10·2	E. McD. Bailey
				M. Campbell
200 metres			20·5	P. Radford
220 yards			20·5	P. Radford
400 metres			45·5	D. Jenkins
440 yards			45·9	R. Brightwell
800 metres		1	46·2	A. Carter
880 yards		1	47·2	C. Carter
1,000 metres		2	18·2	J. Boulter
1,500 metres		3	39·0	P. Stewart
1 mile		3	55·7	A. Simpson
2,000 metres		5	08·2	C. Robinson
3,000 metres		7	47·6	R. Taylor
2 miles		8	24·8	B. Foster
3 miles		12	58·2	D. Bedford
5,000 metres		13	22·2	D. Bedford
6 miles		26	51·6	D. Bedford
10,000 metres		27	47·0	D. Bedford
10 miles		46	44·0	R. Hill
20,000 metres		58	39·0	R. Hill
20,471 metres	1	00	00·0	R. Hill
15 miles	1	12	48·2	R. Hill
25,000 metres	1	15	22·6	R. Hill
30,000 metres	1	31	30·4	J. Alder
120 yd./110 m. hurdles			13·6	D. Hemery
200 metres hurdles (t)			23·0	A. Pascoe
220 yd. hurdles (s)			23·3	P. Hildreth
220 yd. hurdles (t)			23·7	P. Vine
				J. Hogan
400 m. hurdles			48·1	D. Hemery
440 yd. hurdles			50·2	D. Hemery
Steeplechase		8	28·6	D. Bedford

Relays		min.	sec.	
4×100 metres			39·3	British team
4×110 yards			40·0	British team
4×220 yards		1	26·0	London team
4×400 metres		3	01·2	British team
4×440 yards		3	06·5	English team
4×800 metres		7	17·4	British team
4×880 yards		7	17·4	British team
4×1,500 metres		15	06·6	British team
4×1 mile		16	24·8	English team

Field	ft.	in.	metres	
High jump	6	10	2·08	G. Miller
				M. Campbell
Pole vault	16	8¾	5·10	M. Bull
Long jump	27	0	8·23	L. Davies
Triple jump	54	0	16·46	F. Alsop
Shot	64	2	19·56	A. Rowe
Discus	189	11	57·88	J. Watts
Hammer	227	2	69·24	H. Payne
Javelin	273	9	83·44	D. Travis
Decathlon	7,903 points			P. Gabbett

Walking	hr.	min.	sec.	
3,000 metres		11	51·2	P. Nihill
2 miles		13	02·4	S. Vickers
5 miles		34	21·2	K. Matthews
10,000 metres		41	55·6	P. Embleton
7 miles		48	22·2	K. Matthews
20,000 metres	1	28	45·8	K. Matthews
26,037 metres	2	00	00·0	R. Wallwork
30,000 metres	2	30	21·6	D. Thompson
20 miles	2	41	43·8	D. Thompson
30 miles	4	08	11·6	D. Thompson
50,000 metres	4	17	29·8	D. Thompson

Women's Events	min.	sec.	Track
100 yards		10·6	H. Young, D. Hyman
			D. Arden, M. Rand, V. Peat
100 metres		11·3	D. Hyman, D. James
			V. Peat, A. Neil
200 metres		23·2	D. Hyman, M. Critchley
220 yards		23·6	D. Arden
400 metres		52·1	L. Board
440 yards		54·1	D. Watkinson
800 metres	2	01·1	A. Packer
880 yards	2	04·2	A. Smith
1,500 metres	4	12·7	R. Ridley
1 mile	4	37·0	A. Smith
3,000 metres	9	23·4	J. Smith
100 m. hurdles		13·4	C. Bell
200 m. hurdles		26·7	S. Colyear

Relays		min.	sec.	
4×100 metres			43·7	British team
4×110 yards			45·0	British team
4×200 metres		1	33·8	British team
4×220 yards		1	37·6	London Olympiads
4×400 metres		3	30·8	British team
4×800 metres		8	23·8	British team

Field	ft.	in.	metres	
High jump	6	0¾	1·85	B. Inkpen
Long jump	22	2¼	6·76	M. Rand
Shot	53	6¼	16·31	M. Peters
Discus	180	7	55·04	R. Payne
Javelin	182	5	55·60	S. Platt
Pentathlon	5,148 points			M. Peters

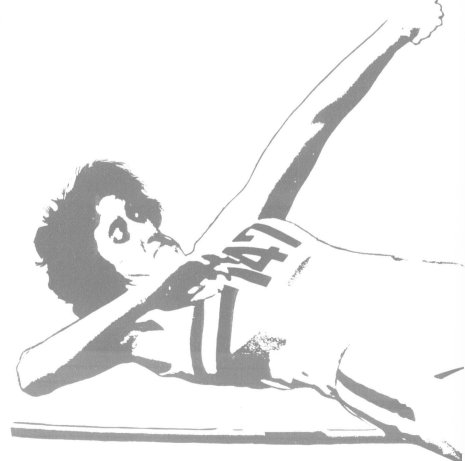

World Records over the decades (Olympic Events)

Men's Events	1921		1931		1941		1951		1961		1971	
	min.	sec.	min.	sec.	min.	sec.	min.	sec.	min.	sec.	min.	sec.
100 metres		10·4		10·3		10·2		10·2		10·0		9·9
200 metres (t)		21·2		21·1		20·6		20·6		20·5		19·8
400 metres		47·4		47·0		46·0		45·8		44·9		43·8
800 metres	1	51·9	1	50·6	1	46·6	1	46·6	1	45·7	1	44·3
1,500 metres	3	54·7	3	49·2	3	47·6	3	43·0	3	35·6	3	33·1
5,000 metres	14	36·6	14	28·2	14	08·8	13	58·2	13	35·0	13	16·6
10,000 metres	30	40·2	30	06·2	29	52·6	29	02·6	28	18·8	27	39·4
4×100 m. relay		42·2		40·8		39·8		39·8		39·1		38·2
4×400 m. relay	3	16·6	3	12·6	3	08·2	3	08·2	3	02·2	2	56·1
110 m. hurdles		14·8		14·4		13·7		13·5		13·2		13·2
400 m. hurdles		54·0		52·0		50·6		50·6		49·2		48·1
Steeplechase			9	21·8*	9	03·8*	8	49·8*	8	30·4	8	22·0

	ft.	in.	m.	ft.	in.	m.	ft.	in.	m.	ft.	in.	m.	ft.	in.	m.	ft.	in.	m.
High jump	6	7¼	2·01	6	8¼	2·03	6	11	2·11	6	11	2·11	7	4½	2·25	7	6¼	2·29
Pole vault	13	5	4·09	14	1½	4·30	15	5¾	4·72	15	7¾	4·77	15	10¼	4·83	18	0	5·49
Long jump	25	3	7·69	26	2¼	7·98	26	8¼	8·13	26	8¼	8·13	27	2	8·28	29	2½	8·90
Triple jump	50	11	15·52	51	1½	15·58	52	6	16·00	52	6¼	16·01	55	10½	17·03	57	1	17·40
Shot	51	0	15·54	52	7½	16·04	57	1	17·40	58	10¾	17·95	65	10	20·06	71	5½	21·78
Discus	156	1	47·58	169	9	51·73	175	0	53·34	186	11	56·97	199	2	60·72	225	5	68·40
Hammer	189	6	57·77	189	6	57·77	193	7	59·00	196	5	59·88	230	9	70·33	250	8	76·40
Javelin	216	10	66·10	239	3	72·93	258	2	78·70	258	2	78·70	284	7	86·74	304	1	92·70
Decathlon				7,036 points			7,421 points			7,453 points			8,063 points			8,417 points		

* World records not recognised till 1954.

Women's Events	1941		1951		1961		1971	
	min.	sec.	min.	sec.	min.	sec.	min.	sec.
100 metres		11·6		11·5		11·2		11·0
200 metres		23·6		23·6		22·9		22·4
400 metres		56·8 (a)		56·0 (a)		53·4		51·0
800 metres	2	16·8	2	12·0	2	04·3	1	58·5
1,500 metres	4	39·6 (b)	4	37·8 (b)	4	25·0 (b)	4	09·6
4×100 metres relay		46·4		46·4		44·3		42·8
4×400 metres relay					3	49·9 (c)	3	29·3
100 metres hurdles						13·3		12·6 (c)

	ft.	in.	m.	ft.	in.	m.	ft.	in.	m.	ft.	in.	m.
High jump	5	5¼	1·66	5	7½	1·72	6	3¼	1·91	6	3½	1·92
Long jump	20	1	6·12	20	6	6·25	21	3¼	6·48	22	5¼	6·84
Shot	47	2¼	14·38	49	3½	15·02	58	4	17·78	67	0½	20·43
Discus	158	6	48·31	175	1	53·37	193	6	58·98	212	10	64·88
Javelin	153	4	46·74	175	2	53·41	195	4	59·55	204	8	62·40
Pentathlon	4,391 points (d)			4,692 points (e)			5,137 points (e)			5,406 points (f)		

(a) First officially recognised by I.A.A.F. in 1957.
(b) First officially recognised by I.A.A.F. in 1967.
(c) First officially recognised by I.A.A.F. in 1969.
(d) Events were, shot, long jump, 100 metres, high jump, and javelin.
(e) Events were, shot, high jump, 80 metres hurdles, long jump, and 200 metres.
(f) 100 metres hurdles substituted for 80 metres.

United Kingdom National Records over the decades

Men's Events	1921			1931			1941			1951			1961			1971		
	min.	*sec.*		*min.*	*sec.*		*min.*	*sec.*		*min.*	*sec.*		*min.*	*sec.*		*min.*	*sec.*	
100 metres		10·6			10·6		:	10·4			10·2			10·2			10·2	
200 metres		21·2			21·2			21·2			20·9			20·5			20·5	
400 metres		48·4			47·6			46·7			46·7			45·7			45·5	
800 metres	1	53·4		1	51·2		1	48·4		1	48·4		1	46·6		1	46·2	
1,500 metres	3	56·8		3	55·0		3	48·7		3	48·0		3	41·1		3	39·0	
5,000 metres	14	48·4*		14	48·4*		14	31·6		14	08·6		13	36·8		13	22·2	
10,000 metres	31	02·4		31	02·4		30	49·0†		30	16·6†		28	52·6		27	47·0	
Steeplechase	10	00·8		9	27·4		9	18·8		9	11·6		8	41·2		8	28·6	
110 m. hurdles		15·2			14·5			14·3			14·3			14·0			13·6	
400 m. hurdles		56·8			53·4			52·2			52·2			51·0			48·1	

	ft.	*in.*	*m.*	*ft.*	*in.*	*m.*	*ft.*	*in.*	*m.*	*ft.*	*in.*	*m.*	*ft.*	*in.*	*m.*	*ft.*	*in.*	*m.*
High jump	6	5	1·95	6	5	1·95	6	5	1·95	6	7½	2·02	6	9	2·06	6	10	2·08
Pole vault	11	9	3·58	12	7½	3·85	13	1½	4·00	13	6	4·12	14	1¼	4·30	16	8¾	5·10
Long jump	24	11¾	7·61	24	11¾	7·61	24	11¾	7·61	24	11¾	7·61	24	11¾	7·61	27	0	8·23
Triple jump	48	11¼	14·91	48	11¼	14·91	48	11¼	14·91	48	11¼	14·91	51	9¼	15·78	54	0	16·46
Shot	48	10	14·88	48	10	14·88	48	10	14·88	54	5	16·58	64	2	19·56	64	2	19·56
Discus	128	4½	39·12	135	6¾	41·32	153	8	46·84	155	3	47·32	181	6	55·32	189	11	57·88
Hammer	169	8	51·72	173	1	52·76	173	1	52·76	183	9	56·00	213	1	64·94	227	2	69·24
Javelin				186	8	56·90	202	2	61·62	210	9	64·24	246	7	75·16	273	9	83·44
Decathlon							5,515 points			6,229 points			6,638 points			7,903 points		

* Converted from 3 miles. † Converted from 6 miles

Women's Events	1941			1951			1961			1971		
	min.	*sec.*		*min.*	*sec.*		*min.*	*sec.*		*min.*	*sec.*	
100 metres		11·9			11·9			11·5			11·3	
200 metres		24·8			24·5			23·6			23·2	
400 metres		56·5			56·5			54·0			52·1	
800 metres	2	14·2		2	14·2		2	06·1		2	01·1	

	ft.	*in.*	*m.*	*ft.*	*in.*	*m.*	*ft.*	*in.*	*m.*	*ft.*	*in.*	*m.*
High jump	5	5¼	1·66	5	7½	1·72	5	8½	1·74	6	0¾	1·85
Long jump	19	2½	5·85	19	2½	5·85	20	9¼	6·33	22	2¼	6·76
Shot	40	6	12·34	41	6¼	12·65	49	1	14·96	53	6¼	16·31
Discus	116	2½	35·42	130	10	39·88	156	6	47·70	180	7	55·04
Javelin	120	9¼	36·82	139	2	42·42	178	7½	54·45	182	5	55·60
Pentathlon				3,953 points			4,679 points			5,148 points		

World's Best Ten up to 1971 (Men)

100 metres

		sec.
J. Hines	USA	9·9
C. Greene	USA	9·9
R. R. Smith	USA	9·9

More than 20 athletes have been credited with 10·0 sec.

200 metres

J. Carlos	USA	19·7
T. Smith	USA	19·8
D. Quarrie	Can	19·8
P. Norman	Aus	20·0
H. Carr	USA	20·1
W. Turner	USA	20·1
M. Fray	Jam	20·1
P. Nash	SA	20·1
C. Glosson	USA	20·1
L. Questad	USA	20·1
J. Bright	USA	20·1
T. Randolph	USA	20·1
M. Dill	USA	20·1
W. Deckard	USA	20·1

400 metres

L. Evans	USA	43·8
L. James	USA	43·9
J. Smith	USA	44·2
V. Matthews	USA	44·4
R. Freeman	USA	44·4
C. Mills	USA	44·4
W. Collett	USA	44·4
T. Smith	USA	44·5
A. Plummer	USA	44·6
O. Davis	USA	44·9
C. Kaufmann	Ger	44·9
M. Larrabee	USA	44·9
T. Lewis	USA	44·9
W. Mottley	Tri	44·9
M. Jellinghaus	Ger	44·9

800 metres

		min. sec.
J. Ryun	USA	1 44·2
P. Snell	NZ	1 44·3
R. Doubell	Aus	1 44·3
W. Kiprugut	Ken	1 44·5
E. Broberg	SA	1 44·7
K. Swenson	USA	1 44·8
F.-J. Kemper	Ger	1 44·9
W. Adams	Ger	1 44·9
W. Bell	USA	1 45·0
D. Malan	SA	1 45·1

1,500 metres

J. Ryun	USA	3 33·1
J. Wadoux	Fr	3 34·0
K. Keino	Ken	3 34·9
H. Elliott	Aus	3 35·6
M. Liquori	USA	3 36·0
M. Jazy	Fr	3 36·3
F. Arese	Ita	3 36·3
J. May	GDR	3 36·4
B. Tummler	Ger	3 36·5
A. de Hertoghe	Bel	3 37·1

5.000 metres

R. Clarke	Aus	13 16·6
D. Bedford	GB	13 22·2
I. Stewart	GB	13 22·8
I. McCafferty	GB	13 23·4
K. Keino	Ken	13 24·2
E. Puttemans	Bel	13 24·6
H. Norpoth	Ger	13 24·8
R. Taylor	GB	13 26·2
S. Prefontaine	USA	13 26·6
M. Jazy	Fr	13 27·6

10,000 metres

R. Clarke	Aus	27 39·4
D. Bedford	GB	27 47·0
J. Vaatainen	Fin	27 52·8
J. Haase	GDR	27 53·4
R. Sharafetdinov	USSR	27 56·4
D. Korica	Yug	27 58·4
M. Haro	Spa	27 59·4
J. Alvarez	Spa	28 01·4
E. Puttemans	Bel	28 01·4
K. Keino	Ken	28 06·4

Steeplechase

K. O'Brien	Aus	8 22·0
V. Dudin	USSR	8 22·2
A. Morozov	USSR	8 23·4
J. Kuha	Fin	8 24·2
M. Zhelev	Bul	8 25·0
J.-P. Villain	Fr	8 25·2
A. Vyerlan	USSR	8 25·4
V. Kudinskiy	USSR	8 26·0
A. Manning	Aus	8 26·2
D. Moravcik	Cze	8 26·2

110 m. hurdles

		sec.
R. Milburn	USA	13·0*
M. Lauer	Ger	13·2
L. Calhoun	Ger	13·2
E. McCullouch	USA	13·2
E. Hall	USA	13·2*
W. Davenport	USA	13·2
T. Hill	USA	13·2
R. Flowers	USA	13·3*
J. Tarr	USA	13·3*
L. Coleman	USA	13·3
M. Walker	USA	13·3*
G. Drut	Fr	13·3

* Distance 120 yards

400 m. hurdles

D. Hemery	GB	48·1
R. Mann	USA	48·5
J.-C. Nallett	Fr	48·6
G. Vanderstock	USA	48·8
W. Collett	USA	48·9
G. Potgieter	SA	49·0
R. Whitney	USA	49·0
G. Hennige	Ger	49·0
J. Sherwood	GB	49·0
J. Akii-Bua	Uga	49·0
W. Williams	USA	49·0

High jump

		ft.	in.	m.
P. Matzdorf	USA	7	6¼	2·29
Ni Chih-Chin	China	7	6	2·29
V. Brumel	USSR	7	5¾	2·28
R. Fosbury	USA	7	4¼	2·24
J. Thomas	USA	7	3¾	2·23
K. Sapka	USSR	7	3¾	2·23
R. Akhmetov	USSR	7	3¾	2·23
I. Major	Hun	7	3¾	2·23
E. Caruthers	USA	7	3½	2·22
C. Johnson	USA	7	3¼	2·21
B. Elliott	USA	7	3¼	2·21
R. Brown	USA	7	3¼	2·21

Pole vault

		ft.	in.	m.
C. Papanikolaou	Gre	18	0	5·49
W. Nordwig	GDR	17	11	5·46
J. Pennel	USA	17	10¼	5·44
K. Isaksson	Swe	17	9¼	5·43
R. Seagren	USA	17	9	5·41
R. Railsback	USA	17	8¾	5·40
C. Schiprowski	Ger	17	8¾	5·40
F. Tracanelli	Fr	17	8¾	5·40
P. Wilson	USA	17	7¾	5·38
H. d'Encausse	Fr	17	7½	5·37

Long jump

		ft.	in.	m.
R. Beamon	USA	29	2½	8·90
R. Boston	USA	27	5	8·35
I. Ter-Ovanesian	USSR	27	4¾	8·35
J. Schwarz	Ger	27	4¾	8·35
R. Coleman	USA	27	0¾	8·25
L. Davies	GB	27	0	8·23
N. Tate	USA	27	0	8·23
W. Stepien	Pol	26	11¼	8·21
K. Beer	GDR	26	10½	8·19
R. Stenius	Fin	26	9½	8·16
P. Shinnick	USA	26	9½	8·16
G. Hopkins	USA	26	9½	8·16
C. Robinson	USA	26	9½	8·16
J. Pani	Fr	26	9½	8·16

Triple jump

		ft.	in.	m.
P. Perez	Cuba	57	1	17·40
V. Saneyev	USSR	57	0¾	17·39
N. Prudencio	Bra	56	8	17·27
G. Gentile	Ita	56	6	17·22
J. Drehmel	GDR	56	2½	17·13
C. Corbu	Rou	56	2	17·12
J. Schmidt	Pol	55	10½	17·03
P. May	Aus	55	10¼	17·02
N. Dudkin	USSR	55	9¾	17·01
P. Pousi	Fin	55	9¼	17·00

Shot

		ft.	in.	m.
R. Matson	USA	71	5½	21·78
H.-J. Rothenburg	GDR	69	3½	21·12
H. Briesenick	GDR	69	2	21·08
N. Steinhauer	USA	68	11¼	21·01
G. Woods	USA	68	0¼	20·73
A. Feuerbach	USA	67	11¾	20·72
D. Long	USA	67	10	20·68
H.-P. Gies	GDR	67	8¾	20·64
D. Hoffmann	GDR	67	7	20·60
W. Komar	Pol	67	5¼	20·55

Discus

		ft.	in.	m.
J. Silvester	USA	224	5	68·40
R. Bruch	Swe	224	2	68·32
T. Vollmer	USA	221	1	67·38
L. Danek	Cze	219	7	66·92
G. Fejer	Hun	219	7	66·92
J. Muranyi	Hun	217	9	66·38
D. Wippermann	Ger	216	2	65·88
M. Hoffman	USA	216	0	65·84
F. Tegla	Hun	214	3	65·30
R. Matson	USA	213	9	65·16

Hammer

		ft.	in.	m.
W. Schmidt	Ger	250	8	76·40
I. Gamskiy	USSR	248	7	75·78
A. Bondarchuk	USSR	247	8	75·48
U. Beyer	Ger	245	9	74·90
R. Klim	USSR	244	6	74·52
R. Theimer	GDR	242	10	74·02
V. Khmyelevskiy	USSR	242	9	74·00
G. Zsivotzky	Hun	242	0	73·76
V. Shchuplyakov	USSR	241	10	73·72
I. Encsi	Hun	240	5	73·28

Javelin

		ft.	in.	m.
J. Kinnunen	Fin	304	1	92·70
P. Nevala	Fin	303	11	92·64
J. Lusis	USSR	301	9	91·98
T. Pedersen	Nor	300	11	91·72
M. Murro	USA	300	0	91·44
M. Stolle	GDR	297	6	90·68
J. Donins	USSR	293	0	89·32
B. Skinner	USA	291	9	88·94
H. Siitonen	Fin	290	1	88·42
A. Nilsson	Swe	287	11	87·76

Decathlon

		points
B. Toomey	USA	8,417
K. Bendlin	Ger	8,319
J. Kirst	GDR	8,279
B. Ivanov	USSR	8,237
R. Hodge	USA	8,230
P. Mulkey	USA	8,155
R. Demmig	GDR	8,130
H.-J. Walde	Ger	8,122
N. Avilov	USSR	8,096
Yang Chuan-kwang	Tai	8,089

World's Best Ten up to 1971 (Women)

100 metres

		sec.
W. Tyus	USA	11·0
Chi Cheng	Tai	11·0
R. Meissner	GDR	11·0
I. Kirszenstein	Pol	11·1
B. Ferrell	USA	11·1
L. Samotyosova	USSR	11·1
M. Bailes	USA	11·1
R. Boyle	Aus	11·1
E. Strophal	GDR	11·1
I. Helten	Ger	11·1
A. Annum	Gha	11·1

200 metres

		sec.
Chi Cheng	Tai	22·4
I. Szewinska	Pol	22·5
R. Stecher	GDR	22·6
R. Boyle	Aus	22·7
M. Burvill	Aus	22·8
B. Ferrell	USA	22·8
J. Lamy	Aus	22·8
G. Balogh	Hun	22·8
E. Strophal	GDR	22·8
W. Rudolph	USA	22·9
M. Bailes	USA	22·9

400 metres

		sec.
M. Neufville	Jam	51·0
Shin Kim Dan	Kor	51·2
N. Duclos	Fr	51·7
C. Besson	Fr	51·7
B. Cuthbert	Aus	52·0
J. Pollock	Aus	52·1
L. Board	GB	52·1
K. Hammond	USA	52·1
H. Seidler	GDR	52·1
A. Packer	GB	52·2
N. Burda	USSR	52·2
Chi Cheng	Tai	52·2

800 metres

		min.	sec.
H. Falck	Ger	1	58·5
V. Nikolic	Yug	2	00·0
G. Hoffmeister	GDR	2	00·8
M. Manning	USA	2	00·9
K. Burneleit	GDR	2	00·9
I. Silai	Rou	2	00·9
J. Pollock	Aus	2	01·0
A. Packer	GB	2	01·1
D. Willis	Aus	2	01·2
L. Board	GB	2	01·4
M. Chamberlain	NZ	2	01·4

1,500 metres

		min.	sec.
K. Burneleit	GDR	4	09·6
T. Pangelova	USSR	4	10·2
G. Hoffmeister	GDR	4	10·3
E. Tittel	Ger	4	10·4
J. Jehlickova	Cze	4	10·7
R. Kleinau	GDR	4	10·9
M. Gommers	Neth	4	11·9
P. Pigni	Italy	4	12·0
A. Veisa	USSR	4	12·5
R. Ridley	GB	4	12·7
I. Keizer	Neth	4	13·0

100 metres hurdles

		sec.
K. Balzer	GDR	12·6
T. Sukniewicz	Pol	12·7
A. Ehrhardt	GDR	12·7
Chi Cheng	Tai	12·8
D. Straszynska	Pol	12·8
V. Bufanu	Rou	12·9
T. Nowak	Pol	12·9
B. Podeswa	GDR	13·0
P. Ryan	Aus	13·0

High jump

		ft.	in.	m.
I. Gusenbauer	Aust	6	3½	1·92
I. Balas	Rou	6	3¼	1·91
A. Lazaryeva	USSR	6	2	1·88
R. Schmidt	GDR	6	1½	1·87
C. Popescu	Rou	6	1½	1·87
V. Chulkova	USSR	6	1½	1·87
S. Hrepevnik	Yug	6	1¼	1·86
M. Hubnerova	Cze	6	0¾	1·85
B. Inkpen	GB	6	0¾	1·85
D. Brill	Can	6	0¾	1·85

continued on page 90

Long jump

		ft.	in.	m.
H. Rosendahl	Ger	22	5¼	6·84
V. Viscopoleanu	Rou	22	4½	6·82
M. Herbst	GDR	22	4¼	6·81
M. Rand	GB	22	2¼	6·76
I. Mickler	Ger	22	2¼	6·76
T. Shchelkanova	USSR	22	1	6·73
M. Antenen	Swi	22	1	6·73
S. Sherwood	GB	22	1	6·73
I. Szewinska	Pol	21	10¾	6·67
T. Talisheva	USSR	21	10¼	6·66

Shot

		ft.	in.	m.
N. Chizhova	USSR	67	0½	20·43
M. Gummel	GDR	65	11½	20·10
A. Ivanova	USSR	63	7½	19·39
M. Lange	GDR	63	2	19·25
H. Friedel	GDR	62	0¼	18·90
T. Press	USSR	61	0	18·59
G. Nyekrasova	USSR	60	8	18·49
I. Friedrich	GDR	60	4	18·39
Y. Korablyova	USSR	59	9	18·21
I. Solontsova	USSR	59	7¾	18·18

Discus

		ft.	in.	m.
F. Melnik	USSR	212	10	64·88
L. Westermann	Ger	209	10	63·96
K. Illgren	GDR	208	10	63·66
T. Danilova	USSR	205	2	62·54
L. Muravyova	USSR	203	0	61·88
C. Spielberg	GDR	202	2	61·64
G. Hinzmann	GDR	201	0	61·26
A. Menis	Rou	200	5	61·08
I. Solontsova	USSR	199	2	60·70
L. Manoliû	Rou	199	1	60·68

Javelin

		ft.	in.	m.
Y. Gorchakova	USSR	204	8	62·40
E. Gryziecka	Pol	203	9	62·10
D. Jaworska	Pol	203	7	62·06
N. Marakina	USSR	203	6	62·04
P. Rivers	Aus	202	8	61·78
E. Ozolina	USSR	201	4	61·38
M. Penes	Rou	199	1	60·68
R. Fuchs	GDR	198	10	60·60
A. Ranky	Hun	198	9	60·58
B. Friedrich	USA	198	8	60·68

Pentathlon

		points
B. Pollak	GDR	5,406
H. Rosendahl	Ger	5,398
L. Prokop	Aust	5,352
M. Herbst	GDR	5,305
I. Mickler	Ger	5,282
V. Tikhomirova	USSR	5,234
M. Peters	GB	5,148
M. Antenen	Swi	5,085
M. Peikert	GDR	5,061
K. Mack	Ger	5,052
D. van Kiekebelt	Can	5,052

United Kingdom Best Ten up to 1971 (Men)

100 metres

	sec.
E. McD. Bailey	10·2
M. Campbell	10·2
R. Sandstrom	10·3
P. Radford	10·3
D. Jones	10·3
B. Jones	10·3
R. Jones	10·3
M. Reynolds	10·3
B. Kelly	10·3

200 metres

	sec.
P. Radford	20·4
R. Steane	20·6
D. Jenkins	20·6
M. Campbell	20·7
R. Banthorpe	20·7
M. Reynolds	20·7
H. Davies	20·8
B. Green	20·8
E. McD. Bailey	20·9
D. Jones	20·9
R. Brightwell	20·9

400 metres

	sec.
D. Jenkins	45·5
R. Brightwell	45·6
A. Metcalfe	45·7
C. Campbell	45·9
M. Winbolt-Lewis	45·9
T. Graham	46·0
J. Wrighton	46·3
E. Sampson	46·5
J. Salisbury	46·5
B. Jackson	46·5

800 metres

	min.	sec.
A. Carter	1	46·2
C. Carter	1	46·3
J. Boulter	1	46·5
D. Johnson	1	46·6
J. Davies	1	46·7
R. Adams	1	46·8
D. Cropper	1	46·9
B. Hewson	1	47·0
M. Rawson	1	47·0
P. Browne	1	47·0

1,500 metres

	min.	sec.
P. Stewart	3	39·0
A. Simpson	3	39·1
I. Stewart	3	39·1
B. Foster	3	39·2
J. Whetton	3	39·4
J. Kirkbride	3	39·5
J. Douglas	3	39·9
J. Boulter	3	40·4
M. Wiggs	3	40·7
W. Wilkinson	3	41·0

5,000 metres

	min.	sec.
D. Bedford	13	22·2
I. Stewart	13	22·8
I. McCafferty	13	23·4
R. Taylor	13	26·2
A. Rushmer	13	29·8
M. Wiggs	13	33·0
M. Baxter	13	35·2
G. Pirie	13	36·8
D. Black	13	37·4
T. Wright	13	39·2

10,000 metres

	min.	sec.
D. Bedford	27	47·0
R. Taylor	28	06·6
L. Stewart	28	11·8
M. Tagg	28	14·8
T. Johnston	28	21·0*
R. Matthews	28	21·4
B. Tulloh	28	22·6*
R. Fowler	28	23·6*
J. Lane	28	24·0
R. Hill	28	25·0*

3,000 metres steeplechase

	min.	sec.
D. Bedford	8	28·6
A. Holden	8	28·8
G. Stevens	8	30·8
M. Herriott	8	32·4
J. Jackson	8	33·0
G. Bryan-Jones	8	33·8
R. McAndrew	8	35·6
E. Pomfret	8	37·0
B. Hayward	8	39·8
D. Camp	8	40·6

110 metres hurdles

	sec.
D. Hemery	13·6
A. Pascoe	13·7
M. Parker	13·9
B. Price	13·9
L. Taitt	14·1
M. Hogan	14·1
S. Storey	14·1
R. Birrell	14·2
R. Morrod	14·2
A. Todd	14·2
D. Wilson	14·2
G. Gower	14·2

* Converted from 6 miles.

400 metres hurdles

	sec.
D. Hemery	48·1
J. Sherwood	49·0
A. Todd	49·9
J. Cooper	50·1
P. Warden	50·7
D. Scharer	50·8
A. Pascoe	50·9
T. Farrell	51·0
C. Surety	51·0
S. Black	51·1

High jump

		ft.	in.	m.
G. Miller		6	10	2·08
M. Campbell		6	9¾	2·08
C. Fairbrother		6	9½	2·07
D. Livesey		6	9½	2·07
P. Taylor		6	9	2·06
D. Wilson		6	8¾	2·05
A. Lerwill		6	8¼	2·04
A. Paterson		6	7½	2·02
P. Wells		6	7½	2·02
J. Ellicock		6	7½	2·02

Pole vault

		ft.	in.	m.
M. Bull		16	8¾	5·10
M. Bryant		16	0	4·87
B. Hooper		15	9¼	4·81
S. Chappell		15	5½	4·71
S. Tufton		15	5	4·70
D. Stevenson		15	4½	4·68
D. Lease		15	3	4·65
M. Higdon		15	1½	4·61
G. Rule		15	1¼	4·60
T. Burton		15	0	4·57

continued on page 91

Long jump

	ft.	in.	m.
L. Davies	27	0	8·23
A. Lerwill	25	11½	7·91
J. Morbey	25	10¾	7·89
G. Hignett	25	6¾	7·79
F. Alsop	25	4¾	7·74
D. Walker	25	2	7·67
P. Reed	25	0¼	7·62
A. Cruttenden	24	10¾	7·59
P. Scott	24	9¾	7·56
G. Williams	24	9½	7·56

Shot

	ft.	in.	m.
A. Rowe	64	2	19·56
G. Capes	63	11	19·48
J. Teale	62	11	19·18
M. Lucking	61	1¼	18·62
M. Lindsay	60	8½	18·50
A. Carter	59	11	18·26
W. Tancred	58	8	17·88
J. Watts	57	8	17·57
B. King	57	1	17·40
W. Fuller	56	4½	17·18

Hammer

	ft.	in.	m.
H. Payne	227	2	69·24
B. Williams	216	8	66·04
M. Ellis	213	1	64·94
I. Chipchase	210	5	64·14
B. Fraser	207	4	63·20
A. Elvin	205	2	62·54
L. Bryce	202	8	61·78
P. Seddon	202	6	61·72
N. McDonald	198	7	60·54
C. Black	196	10	60·00

Decathlon

	points
P. Gabbett	7,903
B. King	7,654
C. Longe	7,451
S. McCallum	7,113
D. Travis	7,067
J. Smith	7,033
D. Clarke	7,002
S. Scott	6,894
D. Hemery	6,893
N. Foster	6,840

Triple jump

	ft.	in.	m.
F. Alsop	54	0	16·46
D. Boosey	53	2½	16·22
A. Wadhams	53	1	16·18
A. Lerwill	52	10	16·10
M. Ralph	52	4¾	15·97
G. Hamlyn	51	11	15·82
J. Vernon	51	8¾	15·77
J. Crotty	51	6½	15·71
G. Webb	51	4	15·64
K. Wilmshurst	51	2¼	15·60

Discus

	ft.	in.	m.
J. Watts	189	11	57·88
W. Tancred	189	6	57·76
A. McKenzie	188	11	57·58
P. Tancred	188	10	57·56
G. Carr	187	0	57·00
R. Hollingsworth	186	0	56·70
M. Cushion	185	6	56·54
D. Roscoe	181	11	55·44
M. Lindsay	181	6	55·32
M. Pharaoh	178	0	54·26

Javelin

	ft.	in.	m.
D. Travis	273	9	83·44
J. FitzSimons	268	9	81·92
J. McSorley	260	0	79·24
J. Greasley	260	0	79·24
C. Smith	255	8	77·94
D. Birkmyre	248	11	75·88
N. Sherlock	247	8	75·48
M. Gavrilovic	246	5	75·12
N. Hart-Ives	245	9	74·90
R. Perkins	245	3	74·76

United Kingdom Best Ten up to 1971 (Women)

100 metres

	sec.
D. Hyman	11·3
D. James	11·3
V. Peat	11·3
A. Neil	11·3
J. Smart	11·5
D. Arden	11·5
J. Paul	11·6
A. Pashley	11·6
H. Young	11·6
J. Simpson	11·6
E. Gill	11·6
J. Hall	11·6
M. Tranter	11·6
D. Ramsden	11·6
H. Golden	11·6
E. Johns	11·6

200 metres

	sec.
D. Hyman	23·2
M. Critchley	23·2
V. Peat	23·3
L. Board	23·4
D. Arden	23·5
M. Tranter	23·5
J. Smart	23·6
D. James	23·6
A. Neil	23·6

400 metres

	sec.
L. Board	52·1
A. Packer	52·2
J. Simpson	52·5
J. Grieveson	53·2
R. Stirling	53·2
M. Green	53·6
D. Watkinson	53·8
J. Roscoe	53·9
M. Hiscox	54·0
A. Bowring	54·0

800 metres

	min.	sec.
A. Packer	2	01·1
L. Board	2	01·4
P. Lowe	2	01·7
R. Stirling	2	02·1
S. Carey	2	02·9
A. Smith	2	03·2
J. Allison	2	03·5
P. Piercy	2	04·1
T. Bateman	2	04·4
J. Jordan	2	05·0

1,500 metres

	min.	sec.
R. Ridley	4	12·7
J. Allison	4	14·8
S. Carey	4	16·2
N. Braithwaite	4	16·8
A. Smith	4	17·3
M. Beacham	4	19·7
G. Tivey	4	21·0
J. Perry	4	22·3
M. MacSherry	4	22·4
C. Haskett	4	23·8
T. Bateman	4	23·8

100 metres hurdles

	sec.
C. Bell	13·4
M. Peters	13·6
A. Wilson	13·6
S. Scott	13·7
P. Jones	13·8
S. Garnett	13·8
S. Hayward	14·0
M. Rand	14·1
I. Powder	14·1
L. Curwen	14·1

High jump

	ft.	in.	m.
B. Inkpen	6	0¾	1·85
L. Hedmark	6	0	1·83
F. Slaap	5	9¼	1·76
T. Hopkins	5	8½	1·74
D. Shirley	5	8½	1·74
A. Wilson	5	8½	1·74
M. Walls	5	8	1·73
R. Watt	5	8	1·73
M. Rand	5	7¾	1·72
G. Hurst	5	7¾	1·72

Long jump

	ft.	in.	m.
M. Rand	22	2¼	6·76
S. Sherwood	22	1	6·73
A. Wilson	21	5¾	6·55
M. Walls	21	1¼	6·43
M. Barton	20	9¾	6·34
B.-A. Barrett	20	8½	6·31
A. Neil	20	7	6·27
A. Stevenson	20	6¾	6·26
J. Caswell	20	5½	6·23
S. Scott	20	5½	6·23

Shot

	ft.	in.	m.
M. Peters	53	6¼	16·31
B. Bedford	51	4¼	15·65
S. Allday	49	9¾	15·18
G. Porter	48	5½	14·77
S. Barrett	46	1¼	14·05
J. Bloss	46	0½	14·03
J. Cook	45	9½	13·96
H. Stuart	45	9	13·94
K. Duckett	45	8	13·92
J. Kerr	45	3	13·79

Discus

	ft.	in.	m.
R. Payne	180	7	55·04
B. Bedford	165	11	50·58
G. Porter	162	11	49·66
H. Atkins	157	6	48·00
S. Allday	156	6	47·70
J. Elsmore	154	8	47·14
J. Frampton	152	4	46·44
J. Fielding	150	5	45·84
M. Giri	150	3	45·80
B. James	150	1	45·74

Javelin

	ft.	in.	m.
S. Platt	182	5	55·60
R. Morgan	177	9	54·18
A. Farquhar	166	9	50·82
S. Spragg	162	8	49·58
A. Williams	162	5	49·50
P. French	158	6	48·30
A. King	157	11	48·14
J. Baker	156	6	47·70
B. Nicholls	156	2	47·60
B. Thomas	155	9	47·48
J. St. Ange	155	9	47·48

Pentathlon*

	points
M. Peters	5,148
A. Wilson	5,037
M. Rand	5,035†
S. Scott	4,786†
M. Walls	4,704
J. Vernon	4,655
J. Honour	4,633
R. Martin-Jones	4,590
S. Hayward	4,473
S. Clelland	4,458

* Pre-1971 scoring table.
† With 80 m. not 100 m. hurdles.

Moment of victory for the author: Harold M. Abrahams wins the
100 metres at the 1924 Paris Olympics, the first European and the
only Englishman to win the event. Conversely, it was the last all-
white Olympic sprint final. Right: Both faces of the gold medal.
Below: Two special plaques commemorating the race. A. E. Porritt
became one of the Queen's surgeons and is now Governor-General
of New Zealand. The four Americans were at one time or other
American champions, and three of them gained world record plaques.

EXICO 1968   OLYMPIC GAM

LES FINAL   MEN'S   400 m

OMEGA   OMEGA   OMEGA   OMEGA   OMEGA   OMEGA

0.0.   0.0.   0.

2   49.0   48.8   48